THE BEACH FISHERMAN'S TACKLE GUIDE

Rods, Reels, Accessories, Rigs
Maintenance, and Tuning

John Holden

THE CROWOOD PRESS

Published by
The Crowood Press
Crowood House, Ramsbury,
Marlborough, Wiltshire,
SN8 2HE, England.

British Library Cataloguing in Publication Data

Holden, John
    The beach fisherman's tackle guide.
    1. Saltwater fishing
    I. Title
    799.1'6   SH457

ISBN 0-946284-25-3

Acknowledgement

Photograph on page eight is reproduced by kind
permission of IPC Magazines.

Phototypesetting by Inforum Ltd, Portsmouth
Printed and bound by Graficromo s.a., Cordoba, Spain

Contents

Author's foreword

If you like surf fishing, you will love tackle making. A steely blank, a handful of rings and a roll of whipping thread are your passport to the fascinating world of rod building. Imagine casting 200 yards with your own tournament rod or fighting those big bass on a super-light carbon fibre rod crafted to your personal design. Who on earth would want to go fishing again with a mass-produced rod?

Tackle making is also great fun in its own right. There is tremendous satisfaction in whipping your own rods, tying traces, even in melting lead over an old gas ring and pouring perfectly aerodynamic sinkers; no factory-fresh reel ever runs as sweetly and controllably as your favourite multiplier tuned and oiled for peak performance; even hooks whipped and sharpened at home seem to catch more fish.

Look around you on the beach. Every season more fishermen like you throw away their old mass-produced casting rods and invest in a fine blank and a kit of accessories. They cast further, catch more fish, and — perhaps the best reason of all for making their own tackle — they enjoy their fishing to the full. Rods are just one item on the list. Almost everything can be made or improved upon with simple tools and a little know-how; and when all is said and done, it is from the garages, kitchens and garden sheds that the world's finest surf casting tackle comes.

John Holden, 1983

Why Build Your Own Rod?

Considering the hundreds of different beach fishing rods on the market, you would think that somewhere along the line any angler could find a ready-made rod that suits him—the right length for casting, properly balanced to handle a realistically wide range of sinker weights and line strengths, smooth and easy to cast with either multiplier or fixed spool reel. Serviceable mass-produced beachcasting rods certainly exist, but most lack the special feel and performance that keen fishermen appreciate.

Once the cheap alternative to production tackle, home-built rods now offer significant advantages. In the high pressure world of tournament casting and long-range beach fishing, specialist blanks reign supreme. You will hardly ever see an expert angler using a standard shop-bought surf rod.

It is not done to save money. The best home-made and custom-built rods cost far more than even the most expensive production rods. Dozens of cheaper blanks are available as well, but the current trend is towards high specification and quality. Production rods, once the first choice of discerning fishermen, are now a cheap option, a starting point for beginners and a refuge for anglers less than dedicated to the sport.

Limitations of production rods

Rod manufacturers must tailor their products for the mass market. One or two models of surf rod each selling thousands are more profitable than twenty specialist rods selling a few dozen each. As a result, mass-produced surf rods are designed to a compromise formula, the aim being to make a rod which is all things to all men. While they never quite hit the target, such rods at least offer reasonable performance and value for money.

Most manufactured surf rods are between 10.5 and 12 feet long, balanced to cast 4–6 ounces, and of medium-fast to fast action. Rings are chosen to perform reasonably well with both fixed spool and multiplier reels. It is assumed that the angler uses an overhead or simple pendulum cast with a maximum range of about 125 yards. Handle diameter and reel spacings are chosen with the 'average' man's physique in mind. In Britain, rods are made exclusively for bottom fishing with natural baits. Elsewhere the emphasis is more likely to be on spinning and lure fishing.

Anglers who cast over 150 yards seldom rely on ordinary production surf rods. Blank and handle

Sluggish fibreglass beachcaster with a sloppy butt. A useless rod typical of the mass-produced tackle industry. Rods like this encourage home building.

are too spongy to transmit full power to the sinker. Rod rings strangle the cast or trap fast-running leader knots. Handles feel too fat or too thin, and the reel is in the wrong place for maximum performance. Bite detection, handling and pulling power may all prove inferior for long range fishing, special techniques and light lines.

Smaller rod building companies are flexible enough to cater for the specialist market. It is economical for them to make a dozen rods at a time, or even to build a one-off model to special order. However, the cost is high because rod assembly is labour intensive. Worse still, small companies seldom offer exclusive blanks and accessories—most blanks are freely available through tackle shops. It does not take long to work out that if you buy an identical blank, rings and handle fittings elsewhere, you can make the same rod for perhaps £30 less. The professionally built rod may be more neatly whipped (Americans say wrapped) and better finished, but it won't cast any farther or hook more fish.

Correct hand spread is essential for good casting. Having the reel in exactly the right place is in itself a good enough reason to build you own surf rod.

Performance versus appearance

Rod appearance and cosmetics are far more important to American and European anglers than to the British. The scene is changing quickly; within ten years everyone might be concerned with a rod's appearance. However, at the moment performance is judged far superior to looks. The attitude among British rod builders, amateur and professional, is that while a nicely finished rod is a bonus, few anglers are willing to spend extra time in achieving it. Fewer still are prepared to pay. Custom rod makers in America would be appalled by the lack of interest shown by the pagan British.

On the other hand, the promise of an extra 15 yards casting range or better bite detection triggers an immediate response. Performance counts heavily on British beaches, casting ability especially so. If a rod maker could guarantee that his products outcast the rest, he would capture the market whatever his prices.

The great advantage of making your own rod is that personal choice is easily accommodated. Should you find that a 12.75 foot surf rod with a 33 inch reel spacing gives you an extra 15 yards casting range, you simply buy a blank and butt, cut them to length and glue the reel seat in the right place. If rod cosmetics appeal to you, it costs only time and patience to indulge your creative instincts. With care you can achieve superb results at home without recourse to specialised equipment and tools. When sheer performance is all that interests you, secure the rings on your new super-casting blank with electrician's tape, and be fishing within an hour of leaving the tackle shop. Dozens of expert casters and competition anglers never both to whip or varnish a new rod.

CHOOSING A BLANK

Surfcasting rods come and go as regularly as the tides ebb and flow. New models appear; old rods die out because styles change or the rod itself can no longer rise to the challenge. Fresh materials arrive on the scene, bring with them the promise of better casting and fishing. After a while, your faithful old beachcaster seems to lose casting power and feels sloppy and imprecise. Even if the rod is healthy, it is easy to talk yourself into changing it.

Anglers are showered with advertisements and information about new rods. Tournament casting and fishing competition results may persuade you to look for another, better blank. Be careful. Though claims for a new rod may well be true, they do not always relate to the way you fish and cast.

High-performance casting blanks are a major source of disappointment. Anglers buy them because they think that rods which exceed 250 yards on the competition field will automatically add 30, 40, even 50 yards to their own casts. It seldom works out that way. It is more likely that the new rod is so long, fierce and rigid that you cannot bend it. Even if it does cast a little further (it is most exceptional to find a blank which alone adds even 10 percent to a caster's performance) the extra yards are hardly worth the effort and expense. The rod is so heavy, stiff and insensitive that you miss bites and lose fish.

I have deliberately singled out casting power for criticism simply because it affects so many fishermen. Thousands of anglers buy a rod that is far too powerful. They are physically unable to compress the blank into its correct casting bend, and as a result they find the rod harsh and unpredictable. No rod casts well unless it is fully compressed to locking point during the casting action.

You must be sure that your casting ability measures up to the blank's specification. If it does not, either reject the blank no matter how great its reputation, or learn to cast harder and more efficiently. The latter course demands hard work and reasonable practice. Ultimately it would pay dividends. If this idea appeals to you, it is probably safe to invest in a blank that is initially a little too powerful and demanding. The big mistake is to suppose that even without extra practice you would eventually come to terms with it. Vast numbers of tournament-grade surf rods on the

secondhand market are proof enough that many anglers finally give up in despair.

Blank selection is so closely allied to casting and fishing skills that anglers who do not understand the principles of rod action and design are at a serious disadvantage. Talk to other anglers, read advertisements and learn what you can about casting and fishing techniques long before you buy that new blank. Rod and blank selection, casting styles and surf tackle combinations are fully covered in this book's companion volume 'LONG DISTANCE CASTING', published by Crowood Press.

Try before you buy

Regardless of your theoretical knowledge of casting, fishing and rod making, there is no real substitute for trying out a new blank before you buy your own. Specifications may appear excellent on paper; the rod casts record distances; perhaps it enjoyed rave reviews in the angling press. All of these are fair indications of a rod's value and ability, but only on the general level. As a rod builder, you should be far more concerned with how the blank measures up to your *personal* requirements. The only way to find out the truth is to test a blank made up to the length and specification you like.

Manufacturers' demonstrations, tackle shows and tournaments provide an opportunity to test

Tournament tackle regulations help determine blank specification. Many of today's best rods are balanced to 0.35–0.40mm line and 5–5.5 ounce sinkers.

blanks and rods. Club members often discover that someone else in the group already owns the blank in question. It is most unusual to be refused a trial. Casting tournaments and fishing competitions are an excellent opportunity to see the latest rods in action. Somebody will almost certainly lend you his rod for a few casts.

Some enlightened retailers and small manufacturers provide trial rods which can be borrowed for a day or two, usually against a cash deposit. Laying your hands on a test blank is much easier than most anglers suppose. Those who complain about not having trial facilities have rarely bothered to look at all the options.

Don't be a manufacturer's guinea pig

Prototype surf blanks involve little expense and time on the manufacturer's part. When suitable materials and mandrels are already available to him, any competent rod designer can transform an idea into a blank within a few hours. Ideas come from the designer himself and through the angling network—tackle shops, angling public and, most important, tournament casters and well-known anglers sponsored by the company. Every good blank factory enjoys strong support from its field staff.

Casting champion Neil Mackellow unleashes a 250 yard cast. Tournament casters and ultra-long range anglers are happy to trade off casting performance against balance and sensitivity.

Feed-back of information and simplicity of prototype blank construction allow designers to stay in close touch with changes in the angling world. Unfortunately, ease of blank making and a strong desire to come up with something new often backfire, and it is the angler who loses . . . and pays.

Tournament champions and prize winning anglers don't have to buy any of their tackle. Someone in the tackle trade will provide whatever they want free in return for the inevitable publicity. In the case of blanks, these men pick and choose from a stream of prototypes made much to their personal specifications. They try out a new rod, sometimes reject it after a week, sometimes keep it for a year. As a one-off exercise, nobody suffers.

Sometimes it happens this way. A tournament caster dreams up a new design of blank which for some reason gives him an extra five yards advantage. He wins a big event. Suddenly, everyone wants a blank like his. Flooded with demands from tackle shops and anglers, the factory churns out new blanks by the score. There are plenty of anglers who will buy a new blank because it is a status symbol. They get a kick from being the first man in their town to own one. Others think the magic will rub off; this new record breaking blank adds 50 yards to *anyone's* cast, surely?

An occasional blank is successful, excellent in every respect, a thoroughly practical fishing and casting rod. However, by the time the new rod hits the tackle shops, our tournament caster has thrown his away. Perhaps his big cast was really due to perfect weather conditions or to different ballraces in the reel. Having used his dream rod for another week, he now finds it too stiff, too soft, too long. Whatever the reason, he needs another new rod for the next tournament.

Shrewd fishermen delay buying the latest wonder rod until it proves itself worth the investment. Rather than jump on the bandwagon, wait and see how anglers in general accept a product. It takes at least six months for some technical problems to emerge. Blanks split or snap after a few hundred casts. Others are useless for practical fishing. A great many feel so heavy and unwieldy that fishermen reject them as fishing rods regardless of how well the blanks cast. Hold back until you see plenty of anglers happily using the new blanks. Even then, do try one before spending your money. These days a bare blank and butt could cost over £100, far too much to risk on an impulse buy.

There are also financial advantages in waiting. Any blank or rod that catches the angling public's imagination will be copied by other manufacturers. Copyright and patent are almost worthless in fishing rod manufacture. It is easy to take apart a blank, see how it works and make a copy which exactly parallels the original's action and power. Good designers often manage to improve the performance, and they certainly try to reduce the price. In the long run, you could buy a better blank for a lot less money.

Blank quality

Physical dimensions apart, most blanks look similar. It is extremely difficult for the inexperienced to differentiate between good and bad. Glassfibre, carbonfibre (graphite) and composites of the two are available in a wide range of specifications. Fibres and the resins which bind them are difficult to assess outside the laboratory. Looks can actually create a deliberately false impression of blank quality. A good coat of high-gloss finish over a lick of cheap paint makes an inferior product seem highly desirable. Lying alongside it, a vastly superior but unglossed blank looks like a fake, and a very expensive one at that.

Carbonfibre rods are a perfect example. Cheap Far Eastern blanks look nice and cost next to nothing. American and British blank makers cannot compete with them on price alone. The tragedy is that few anglers realise how great are the differences between good and bad carbonfibre materials. To the man in the street, all carbonfibre is the same. Presented with a cheap import and a nationally-produced blank of similar external appearance, he looks no further than the price tag. Why pay three times as much for Fenwick, Lamiglas, Bruce & Walker, Conoflex or Zziplex when you can get a Taiwan rod, made up and ready to fish, for a few pounds or dollars?

Use quality products alongside the rest and you immediately see and feel an enormous difference in balance, performance and sensitivity. On top of that, you can bet that a cheap rod will be dead and buried inside two years. Choice is limited as well. Churning out such vast numbers of rods and blanks, the Far East cannot afford to cater for specialists. The range may include only three or four surfcasting blanks, all around the 11–12 foot mark.

Fenwick and Conoflex manufacture literally hundreds of specialist saltwater blanks. There is an excellent chance of finding precisely the specification you want. The whole idea of building your own rod is to escape the prison of mediocre design, so why trap yourself for the sake of a little extra

Not all production rods are bad. Old ABU models are quite good. Now obsolete, they are still sought after on the second hand market by custom builders who refurnish the bare blank with modern rings and handles.

expense? After you add the cost of rings, fittings and accessories, and the hours spent whipping and varnishing the rod, it simply does not make sense to buy inferior blanks. Stick to the big names unless you have good reason to change.

On the other hand, do not overlook that new blank factory just opened down the road. It could be the answer to your prayers. Wait six months to see how other anglers feel about their product—it is always wise to let somebody else take the preliminary risks. The danger is that the new rods could become so popular that eventually you find yourself on the end of a long waiting list.

Finding a new blank

It is physically impossible for an ordinary tackle shop to stock every model of blank. Expect to shop around for your new rod. In most areas, blank manufacturers limit the number of tackle retailers who sell their products. It is better for trade and ensures faster service and more useful advice. With so many blanks on the market, very few dealers could hope to have a thorough knowledge of them all. You can discover the name and address of your nearest specialist dealer either by checking through the angling magazines and newspapers or by writing or calling the factory itself. Some manufacturers will supply direct in

Casting tournaments and beach matches are the best places to see new rods. If you ask nicely, most anglers are happy to tell you about their tackle, and perhaps they will let you try it.

case of difficulty. The best have either their own showrooms or other demonstration and trial facilities. A blank maker may occasionally be willing to make you a special one-off design. It will much depend on his workload, and everything hinges on whether he has a suitable steel mandrel.

Good blanks withstand a beating year in, year out. Over a very long period—say five years—a high quality blank used carefully and within its limits shows little sign of deterioration. Some blanks soften a little, others tend to grow slightly harsh because resins harden and lose their flexibility. However, deterioration is so slight that you never notice it. As for breaking in half without warning, there is little to worry about unless you are an exceptionally bad caster who continually overloads his blank. Experience shows that if a rod is going to break, it will almost certainly do so within its first year and probably within the initial three months. All of this makes a secondhand blank worth considering .

Fishing magazines and local newspapers are full of small advertisements for secondhand rods and blanks. These are brand new blanks which the owner never got around to building; rods two or

three months old that didn't suit him; and old rods no longer manufactured but still sought after. Prices are invariably a fraction of new. Even secondhand rods from a tackle shop can be quite a bargain. From a keen home-builder's point of view, the state of a blank is all that matters. However well the existing rod is built and fitted out, he will strip off rings and handle, scrape the blank clean and start again.

It can be worth taking a gamble. To start with, you can be sure of a few test casts before you buy the rod. Nobody selling a rod ever turns down such a request. A smooth-casting rod free from obvious damage to the blank is a sound investment. If the rod is in a bad state—except for the blank of course—you may be able to beat the price right down. You can also afford to take a chance on action and power. Should the blank eventually prove unsuitable, just get rid of it. Cunning rod traders make a profit on the deal. A quick check through my back issues of Angler's Mail Swop Shop column reveals that most saltwater rods described as in good, perfect or as-new condition are advertised for around half to two-thirds of list price. And that is before you start haggling.

10

Rod Building: Blanks

ONE-PIECE BLANKS

In theory a blank without joints should be stronger than one with spigots or ferrules, and it should perform better as well. In practice, any high quality blank correctly cut and jointed is just as strong, casts and fishes equally well, and is far easier to transport and store. Most high-performance rods for casting and fishing are manufactured in sections.

Should your chosen blank be one-piece, do not rush to cut it. There is no overwhelming reason why some blanks should not be cut, but do bear in mind a couple of important points before you start using a hacksaw. Wall thicknesses and diameters are calculated so that unless a cut is made in exactly the right spot—which may not be the centre—a rod is seriously weakened. Even if a blank is safe to cut, you must not glue in any old spigot. Wall thickness, taper, length and the material of the spigot itself must be absolutely correct, otherwise the rod literally tears itself apart.

Cutting and jointing blanks is a highly skilled job. High-performance surf blanks with fast taper and stiff butt are very much at risk. Slower action rods are less susceptible, but in the long run they too may split the outer walls or snap the spigot. There is only one safe answer: before buying the blank, ask the manufacturer if it can be sectioned, and if so at which points. The factory or dealer might supply a special plug for your particular model.

SECTIONAL BLANKS

The vast majority of surf rods are now constructed in two equal-length sections or as long tips and detachable handles. While excellent casting and fishing rods exist in telescopic and multi-section format, modern designers turn the spotlight on the two piece formula which offers a greater scope for performance, lightness and cheaper manufacture. One piece rods are under heavy fire from the tackle trade because they are so difficult to ship and store. It costs as much to send one blank as twenty; express delivery services like UPS and Securicor refuse to handle long packages anyway.

The long-tip/detachable butt formula gains rapid support from blank dealers, retailers and anglers. A handful of well chosen blanks cover all power and length requirements, whereas with equal-length section rods it is necessary to offer a big range of options to cover the market. One long tip plus three or four handle options take the place of a dozen or more conventionally sectioned rods.

Equal-length sections should not be dismissed. At the bottom end of the market are bare blanks and semi-built rods which offer reasonable performance and price. Choice of length, action and power are severely limited, which makes these blanks interesting to anglers looking for the cheapest possible way into beach fishing. At the other extreme, superb carbonfibre blanks cut and jointed in the centre are available for specialist angling and long-range casting. They tend to be few and far between, and prices are high.

Rod length alteration

Rods made in two equal length (or close-to-equal) sections cannot easily be modified. A 12 foot surf blank might withstand trimming back by 6 inches at the butt or 2–3 inches at the tip; but apart from that, you are restricted to the designer's limits. Adding a few inches to the butt is sometimes an acceptable method of lengthening a rod. Apart from loss of balance, the biggest danger is that the relative position of the joint has now shifted towards the tip ring. Joint stress is severely increased and spigot or blank walls may fail. Even if a rod does retain its strength, casting performance drops because the spigot weight reduces rod tip recovery speed.

A long tip is capable of accepting varying lengths of handle. Assuming you pick the correct power and action of blank, overall rod length with the standard 7.5–8.5 foot tips can lie anywhere between 11 and 14.5 feet. Within that range lies adequate scope for pendulum, South African, overhead and back cast styles. It is surprising how versatile some blanks can be.

Conoflex Cod 5's and 6's could be made up into an 11.5 foot pendulum rod to cast 4 ounces, or extended at the butt and trimmed a little at the tip to produce a back-cast rod 14 feet long and powerful enough to cast between 6 and 8 ounces. At the other extreme, the Zziplex Dream Machine, Fenwick Surfstik 5 and Conoflex 240T pendulum blanks are better kept around 11.5 feet long for casting 5–5.5 ounces. Just an inch or two cut from the end of the rod would ruin

Two-piece rods offer good casting and fishing along with easy carriage and storage. The only snag is that two-piece rods are available in relatively few lengths, actions and powers.

performance and in some cases make the rod too harsh and vicious to use.

Cutting back the tip of any blank must be approached with caution. The best advice is *not* to cut unless there are overwhelming pressures to do so, or the blank is one which incorporates variable length as a design feature. Some blanks can be progressively cut back to accommodate a wide sinker range. A full length blank balanced to 5 ounces may produce better results with 6 ounces if 3 inches of tip are sliced off. Taking off another 2 inches raises the ideal sinker weight to 8 ounces.

An individual angler's casting power plays its role. Blanks built for 5 ounce casting under normal conditions may respond better to very hard casts with the same weight if an inch or two are cut off the tip. See how other anglers fare after cutting back their rods. Talk to tournament casters as well; they are more likely than anyone to take a hacksaw to the blank. Tip reduction is an area of rod building where it pays to learn by others' experience.

Rod length has enormous bearing on casting distance and control. There seems no practical difference between similar rods cut, say, 11.5 and 11.75 feet long. How could 3 inches alter a pendulum blank's performance? Casters who struggle to achieve 100 yards feel nothing. Moderately good casters who drop their baits around the 130 yard mark might notice a slight difference in handling; perhaps one rod would cast marginally farther.

Beyond 175 yards those 3 inches could add or cut 25 yards from maximum performance; they might require at least a half-ounce change in sinker weight; and they will almost certainly affect reel position, sinker drop and power flow during the cast. Length itself is important, but the altered characteristics of a cut blank also play a part, especially if the 11.5 foot model was produced by cutting 3 inches from the original tip.

Spigots and joints

The position and security of a joint depends on the length and construction of the blank. Slow tapered rods for bass fishing, casting lures and short-to-medium range beach casting are versatile in this respect. Reputable manufacturers offer a range of suitable blanks in the 11–13 foot range, in glassfibre, carbonfibre and composites. Each blank is cut and jointed by overlap or plug spigot. There is no advantage in placing the joint towards the

12

Short aluminium butt and flexible carbonfibre blank—just the right combination for turbot fishing from the rocks.

A rod rest means that you can afford to use quite a heavy, powerful blank with a high casting performance. As a general rule, very powerful casting rods are too unwieldy to hold all day.

butt; the centre or somewhere close by is perfectly all right. Such rods lack all-out casting power but are light, well balanced, sensitive and easy to use. According to design, they are a good choice for all-round and specialist short range work. Spigot and joint failure are unusual in good quality blanks. A full length blank of this type is manageably slim at the butt and therefore requires no special handle provision.

Where casting power heads the list of blank characteristics, rod designers have two roads to travel. The flexible tip/stiff butt, fast action rod can be built either by using a steeply tapered mandrel and thin blank walls, or by reducing the mandrel taper and compensating for the lower diameter (and its associated lack of stiffness) by a substantial increase in glassfibre or carbonfibre thickness. There are plus and minus factors in each design.

Joint placement and construction are very important, yet some rod manufacturers and custom builders ignore them. As a result, many fishermen buy blanks which are fragile and unreliable. Some snap in half on the first powerful cast; at best they have little insurance against abuse or accidental overload.

Measure down 5.5–6 feet from the tip ring of a thin wall/steep taper rod like the Conoflex Cod 5 or 6, and you find that the external diameter is about $\frac{1}{2}$–$\frac{5}{8}$ inch. Walls are thin, giving plenty of room inside the blank for a sturdy spigot. Any blank of this kind is ideal for making up into a rod of two equal length sections. The only cause for concern is the length and wall thickness of the spigot itself. The risk is that the spigot may harm the rod.

The mid-area of a fast-action casting rod is subject to considerable strain. It is also the region of maximum acceleration during the final stage of a big cast. The blank must be strong, but it must bend as well. A rigid spigot tends to lever apart the walls of the blank. Thus, the size of the spigot must be carefully calculated to blend in. All the best rods are designed and built as a unit, and most come from the factory with spigot cut, ground and glued in place.

Thick wall/slim diameter blanks are better left uncut. At the 5.5–6 foot point, walls are substantial and the outside diameter under $\frac{1}{2}$ inch. The central hole, which determines spigot diameter, is too narrow for safety. In this case the blank breaks its spigot. Should a spigot hold together, casting power is severely reduced because the joint flexes more than the surrounding blank and thus forms a soft spot in the action.

With most kinds of surfcasting rods it is neater

13

to run the blank over a full 8 feet or so and use a detachable butt. Although a few production rods still feature a thick walled blank jointed in the middle by a weak spigot, it is now uncommon to find a specialist blank made in this way. Anglers and manufacturers are wise to the problem . . . too many of the early blanks broke after a dozen casts.

Spigots work extremely well on all long-tip blanks, fast or slow tapered and, unless there is a manufacturing error or faulty material, premature failure is rare. The only precaution is to whip the final 4–6 inches of the blank to prevent splitting. An alternative is to dispense with the spigot and instead use a handle which pushes into the bottom of the tip. Glassfibre, aluminium alloy and carbonfibre butts can be attached this way provided diameters and wall thicknesses are suitable. The overlap area is better ground in the factory, but with care can be produced by hand tools.

The Feralite joint in Fenwick's Surfstik series is particularly neat because upper and lower sections of rod are made on special mandrels which provide for a tapered overlap. By avoiding the need to grind the handle to shape, Fenwick preserve full wall thickness and rods are actually stronger than if they were made in single-piece form.

Where blank diameter is less than that of its chosen handle, you can opt for a reverse spigot. The outside wall of the tip is ground to slide into the butt. Reasonable wall thickness is necessary both sides, and the inside of the butt should be parallel or even reverse tapered. The idea works best with thickwall/slim diameter tips and aluminium alloy butts. As an alternative, glue the butt into the handle. Modern epoxy adhesives are strong enough to take up a reasonable amount of sloppiness between the two sections, so that it is seldom necessary to grind the joint to a precision fit. With thick adhesive and a few yards of string to fill the gap you can bond a 1 inch blank into 1–1.25 inch alloy tube.

Blank design and handle limitations
Fast taper mandrels increase in diameter so quickly that were you to make a blank even 11 feet long, the butt would be too thick to hold. Some of the fastest mandrels used for surf rods are uncomfortably fat by the 8 foot point and would exceed 1.75 inches in diameter at 12 feet. The only practical answer is to cut the blank above the handle, then insert or spigot on a parallel or slow-tapered butt more suited to the average man's hands. Nothing is lost if the rod is made on the long tip/detachable butt theme.

If the rod is jointed in the centre, you still must add a separate butt, though in this case it is standard practice to glue it permanently in position. Properly done, it is a satisfactory but expensive modification. The rod costs more, and it is heavier. Sometimes the extra joint's weight detracts from feel, balance and power.

Fast, powerful blanks built on slower tapers are in theory quite easy to extend to 12 or 13 feet with no need for a separate butt. You can build medium power rods in this way, so why not a high-performance surf blank?

Butt rigidity is the limitation. Handle walls would be so thick that the rod would be heavy and dull to cast. The mass of glass alone would boost handle diameter beyond manageable limits. However, the principle is upheld with carbonfibre blanks because the material is so stiff, even in lower diameter/fairly thin wall construction. Unfortunately such rods are very expensive, but they do represent the state of the art in rod building. Again, regardless of material, the practical alternative is to curtail the main blank at the 7.5–8 foot mark and add on a separate butt.

Blank materials
Glassfibre remains the most popular blank material of all, but is fast losing ground to

Small dabs are all you can expect from some European beaches. Light carbonfibre rods help anglers make the best of a bad job.

14

semi-carbon and carbonfibre. Glassfibre is available in a variety of grades, cloth weaves and resin systems. As far as the angler is concerned, the precise specification matters little. Few if any ordinary glassrods are better than the rest except in taper and wall construction. For powerful casting a sloppy blank of the finest materials is far inferior to a fast-action rod of cheaper specification. On the other hand, a super-fast rod of premium-grade material is useless if your style of fishing demands a slow action blank with plenty of feel and flexibility in the lower half. Judge a blank by length, speed and general construction. Pay more attention to the maker's name than to the formula of his materials; most good designers won't tell you the innermost secrets of their products anyway.

The important exception is 'S' glassfibre, which is a much tougher, faster and more powerful material than ordinary 'E' grade glassfibre. Few manufacturers use it because it is much more difficult to work with. Fenwick and others—nearly all of them American—who have mastered 'S' glassfibre have proved it to be a perfect material for surf rods, especially for those which combine high performance with angling versatility.

Carbonfibre is taking a stranglehold on beach fishing and casting. In time it will dominate the market. Materials used in rod manufacture are a spin-off from the aerospace industry, which is fast moving from glass to carbonfibre. Consequently glassfibre must become scarcer and more expensive while carbonfibre drops in price. Soon the price difference between carbon and glass rods will fall to the point where nobody buys glassfibre rods.

Carbon is much lighter, faster, more precise and more sensitive than other rod materials. Other Space Age products like boron and silicon carbide may eventually challenge its supremecy for sea fishing, but at the moment it reigns supreme. From the designer's point of view the material is still in its infancy. We have long appreciated its theoretical advantages, but early work was plagued by breakages and poor results. Early production blanks and rods created an aversion to carbonfibre that still exists today, despite the massive strides taken since 1980. Today's carbon rods are far superior in every respect. The remaining snags are cost and selection. Carbonfibre rods are only available in a narrow range of lengths, strengths and actions. As more anglers become familiar with the material, carbonfibre will take over on beach and tournament field. If you have never tried a *good* carbonfibre blank, make an effort to do so. It is most unlikely you would ever want to fish again with glassfibre or even semi-carbon.

Semi-carbon is a bastard form of rod building in which carbon is used to stiffen the lower sections of a glassfibre blank. It adds rigidity, reduces weight and diameter, and thus boosts casting power. As such it is a valuable option, but it is not a substitute for a real carbonfibre rod. Semi-carbon is little more than a neat and cost-effective way to improve ordinary glassfibre. Great claims have been made for its casting performance, but it is the butt of a blank which really holds the secret of longer casts. Semi-carbon is also inferior to 'S' glassfibre in terms of balance, weight and fishing sensitivity; although as casting rods they are on a par.

Rod Building: The Basics

Rod building falls neatly into two stages: basic assembly of the blank and handle, followed by ring whipping and general finishing. Neither requires special tools or great skill, but it still pays to work to a logical plan. With standard blanks this is simply done because ring spacings, handle length and reel seat position are fairly sure to fall into a well known pattern. Specialist rods are not so easy to assess. Wise rod builders know that somewhere along the line every new rod must be tested. If you can arrange to do this before the final whipping, gluing and varnishing, so much the better. There is nothing worse than spoiling a brand new rod by moving the rings or reel seat. No matter how carefully you work, an altered rod will never look as neat as the original.

Most anglers hold the view that rod building should be kept as simple as possible. Handle assembly, spigot whipping, rod rings and varnishing are basic steps in construction, and nowhere along the line should even the raw beginner hit trouble. A first rod never looks perfect, but with care you can be sure it will at least do its work and last a long time. Patience is more valuable than talent.

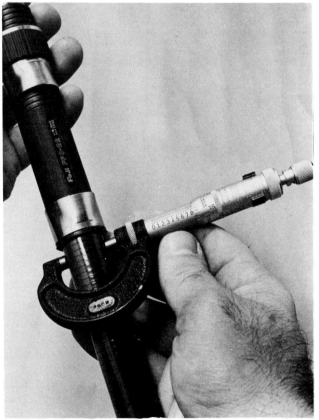

Check the blank diameter and pick the reel seat which most easily marries to it. It is useless to make do—if the reel is in the wrong place, casting suffers.

Your headaches begin when various components do not match up. If you know where the reel seat should fit on the handle, it is easy to measure blank diameter at that point, choose a reel seat of precisely the right size or very close to it, slide it on and apply adhesive. But suppose you did not check the position and diameters beforehand. There is an excellent chance that either the reel seat will sit too high on the handle, or will be so sloppy a fit that glue alone cannot make up the difference.

The logical answer is to change the reel seat. But it seldom works out that way in real life. If the tackle shop were close by, most anglers would indeed exchange the seat; but as more often happens shops are far away (lots of rods and accessories are bought by mail order), and the urge to finish your new rod is just too strong anyway. The rod ends up with its reel in the wrong place, which ruins casting performance, or it is bodged together with packing strips and masses of glue. After a month's hard fishing, the reel seat loosens and skids around the blank as you wind in.

Silly mistakes need not happen; but there are few newcomers to rod building who sail through the early days unscatched. RULE ONE, then, is to make sure that *all* the parts are compatible *before* it is too late to alter the building plan. RULE TWO is equally important. Make sure that all the parts for your new rod are *available*.

Take rod rings for example. The world is littered with millions of rod rings of all shapes, sizes and materials. All a rod builder needs for his new blank is one complete set, tip to butt. Surely no problem? If you need, for instance, 12mm tip, 10mm, 12mm, 16mm, 20mm, 25mm and 30mm intermediates, make sure you have them all in hand *before* you start building. Should there be some doubt about the numbers—say you think the rod might need an extra 12mm ring—buy it *now*.

The unwritten law of ring supply guarantees that the one you particularly want is never in stock next week. Try it and see. The same applies to the original set: if the tackle dealer has them all bar one—"but I can get one for you in a couple of days"—watch your step. I bet it does not arrive for three months.

Advanced builders know all about erratic supply and ill-matched accessories. Gradually they accumulate enough spare rings and fittings to overcome most snags. You learn with experience

ROD BUILDING: SUGGESTED FLOW OF WORK

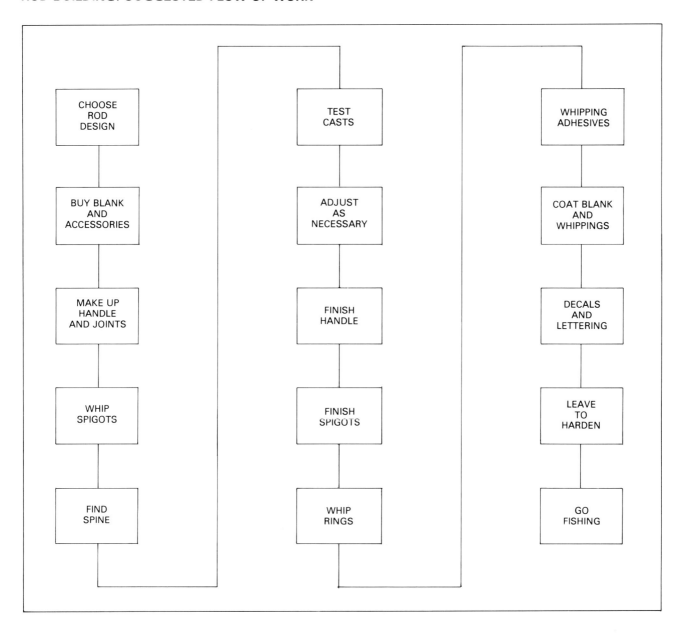

to modify things to fit. Blanks can be built up to take a standard reel seat. Reel seats are sleeved, or in some cases reamed out. Hand grips and butt caps are stretched and shrunk to fit. You can even learn to make special joints and handles. Such versatility takes time and experience. To start with, take the easy way out. Buy the bits, slide them into position, and run through the whipping, gluing and varnishing. Some anglers prefer to buy a semi-built rod with handle and fittings already in place. All you do is whip on the rings and brush on a gloss finish.

Making a start

The flow diagram highlights various stages in making a surf rod. The sequence of events is based on practical experience more than anything. There is no right and wrong way to assemble rods, but

there are ways to save time and disappointment, especially with more complex designs. Most errors are so obvious that you kick yourself afterwards. The classic one is to whip on a butt ring and then discover that you cannot slide on the reel seat and hand grips.

STAGE 1

Find out as much as you can about suitable blanks. Try as many as possible, and ask the tackle shop and manufacturer for technical literature and building suggestions. Pick the blank you like best and check it for obvious surface damage. Unless the rod comes in two sections with a spigot in place, make sure the manufacturer supplies a separate spigot so that you can make up your own butt. Most single-piece blanks arrive complete or are designed to fit inside a parallel butt tube.

Choose whipping thread, rings and handle components. Buy the necessary varnish or two-part epoxy coat, a pack of adhesive (Araldite standard and rapid are both excellent) and a stick of hot-melt glue for the tip ring. Store the kit indoors while you build the rod. Dust ruins a good finish. Condensation and cold are a menace. Glue takes forever to harden. Varnish will not flow. Everything is wringing wet.

The household tool kit provides most of the essentials:
Hacksaw
Craft knife or razor blade
Scissors
Sellotape or Scotch tape
Medium-cut file
Candlewax
Wet-and-dry carborundum paper, medium and fine grades
Chalk or grease pencil
Ajax or similar scouring powder
Methylated spirit.

STAGE 2: For single-piece blanks without butts

Butt materials available:
Glassfibre
Aluminium alloy tube
Glassfibre/alloy laminate
Carbonfibre/alloy laminate
Glassfibre/carbonfibre laminate
Carbonfibre
Boron/carbonfibre laminate

For any given surf blank there are always several butt options. In general it pays to conform to the designer's recommendations, and to use his chosen jointing method. If a spigot is required, be sure to order it along with the blank so it can be accurately ground and fitted in the factory.

The trend is for manufacturers to supply butts which complement the main blank. Sometimes you have a choice of two or three materials, and there are diameters and stiffnesses to suit preferred rod length. An 8 foot semi-carbon tournament tip made up to 11.5 feet overall would generally be supplied with either a high tensile aluminium alloy butt of 1–1.25 inch diameter or a carbon butt (pure or laminated) of roughly the same dimensions but with a far higher casting performance. The same blank made in 13 foot South African style might feature an aluminium alloy butt between 1.125 and 1.25 inch diameter. Its carbon alternative is slimmer and lighter, far more powerful and precise ... and extremely expensive.

According to your purse, casting ability and personal preference, choose whichever option makes sense. The great advantage of single-piece blanks is that should the original butt prove inadequate you can buy another. Two butts—short and long—plus a single tip is an excellent combination for anglers who like to experiment or who choose their casting styles (and therefore their rod lengths) according to season, weather, sinker weight and species of fish. It is quite common to use an 11.5 foot rod for everyday fishing, and to plug in a longer butt (overall rod length say 12.5 feet) for tournaments and extremely long range beach work.

Balanced performance and easy jointing are key factors in butt selection. Take advice before you buy. Most fishermen are content to use the manufacturer's recommended butts. Experimenters and rod building fanatics stray from the easy path. Careful selection based on experience and individual preference may well result in the perfect rod for you. However, consider the disadvantages as well: substantial modifications to butt and tip may be necessary; and full workshop facilities including a lathe and belt sander are often indispensible.

Full power on the tournament court. Ordinary rod handles neither stand the strain nor give the best performance. Alloy and carbonfibre are preferred.

Which butt material is best?

Given an entirely free choice, most surf fishermen would do better with carbon fibre butts, which are superior in all respects except price. However, more practical advice is to use a butt material at least as good as that of the tip. The world's finest blank attached to a cheap handle would be outclassed by an ordinary tip pepped up by a sophisticated butt.

Some anglers and custom rod builders think the tip is more important than the butt, and they resent paying extra cash for, say, carbonfibre/glassfibre laminate rather than low-grade aluminium alloy. They are wrong. One cast with the better material would convince them. However, it is wrong to dismiss other handle materials without first examining their strengths and weaknesses.

Glassfibre

Parallel wall or slow-tapered glassfibre butts offer reasonable performance with lower-grade surf blanks. There is no point using glass butts with any tip except plain glassfibre. An ordinary 'E' glass butt is no match for an 'S' glass tip.

Glassfibre butts are at their best with medium-fast surf rods and are most often encountered on two equal-piece blanks. Choice of handle does not even arise. On the fast-action single tip design, detachable or glued-in parallel glassfibre butts are a poor choice for high performance casting and fishing. It is virtually impossible to make them stiff enough.

Aluminium alloy tube

Metal tube offers a significant boost in butt stiffness, without imposing too much of a weight handicap. Unfortunately, it is a brutal material which ruins the feel and delicacy of many blanks. Casting distances are much improved, but at some cost in cast control.

Aluminium alloy tube is inelastic compared to glassfibre and carbonfibre. It is a source of rigid leverage and little else. However, it works very well for many casters and fishermen. Assuming that length, diameter and wall thickness of the tube are well chosen, you can enjoy first class casting and pleasant enough general fishing. It is not a material for light surf and lure rods, but certainly comes into its own for heavy sinkers and tournaments.

Alloy is also very cheap. You can afford to buy a longer than normal butt. Test the rod in over-length form, and trim the butt back with a hacksaw, inch by inch, until you arrive at the perfect rod. Very often a rod 3–6 inches longer than normal works better than you would have imagined. Sometimes a shorter than average rod gains distance. It costs little to find out, and should you accidentally over-trim the butt (or wish to lengthen an existing alloy handle) just buy a few inches of smaller diameter tube and push it into the original.

Low cost and easy replacement are useful in the longer term as well. The serious problem with alloy is that butts seldom last more than two years without succumbing to salt corrosion. Sometimes they snap in half without warning, especially if the metal is covered in shrink tube.

There are many grades of aluminium alloy. Best for rod making are HE30 and HT15, drawn seamless tube. These specifications are British Standards which have direct equivalents elsewhere. Engineering text books and aluminium manufacturers supply a conversion chart. HE30 is ordinary high-tensile dural available from non-specialist industrial tubing suppliers and through the tackle trade. It is more than good enough for general rod building.

In ardous conditions HT15 grade alloy is better still. Relatively expensive (though far cheaper than carbonfibre) and harder to find, it is the material of choice for 11.5–11.75 feet pendulum casting rods used with the reel in the upper position for 5–6 ounce sinkers. It may be used for any rod though, and generally you can afford to use one step lower external diameter than necessary with HE30. The best suppliers are airframe and aerospace alloy factors.

Suggested diameter/wall thicknesses for 4–6 ounce surf rods:
Up to 40 in. butt or 11.5 ft. rod, high reel position—*1 in.*/16SWG HT
Up to 40 in. butt or 12 ft. rod, reel high or low—*1.125 in.*/16SWG HE
Pendulum rods, 40 in.—plus butt, reel high or low—*1.125—1.25 in.*/16SWG HE
Back cast rods 13.5 ft.—14.5 ft. reel low—*1.25–1.375 in*/16SWG HE

Composite and laminated butts
A few layers of glassfibre wrapped around aluminium alloy tube one size slimmer than normally standard for the rod, offer protection from permanent bends and introduce a fair degree of control without sacrificing too much speed and leverage. Laminated butts are quite pleasant to fish with, fairly light and unlikely to be eaten away by saltwater. Prices are quite competitive as well. In all, a recommended compromise for medium performance surf rods.

Lamination works well for carbonfibre and alloy. The object is to raise casting power without spending the earth. Three or four wraps of carbonfibre are sufficient to boost casting range by perhaps 5 percent—of little consequence in fishing but useful on the tournament field.

Composites of carbonfibre and glassfibre are marginally better than the above laminate, and represent a useful step closer to pure carbon

without incurring a massive price penalty. The ratio of carbon to glass varies between manufacturers, as do perforrmance, balance and cost. Although hardly lighter than the best alloy laminates—and sometimes significantly heavier—composites do cast farther and, more important, are far smoother than any lower grade of butt material. They are especially good with semi-carbon tips. All lengths, diameters and wall thicknesses are available, mostly direct from the blank factory, spigotted where necessary and matched to a specific blank, rod length and casting style.

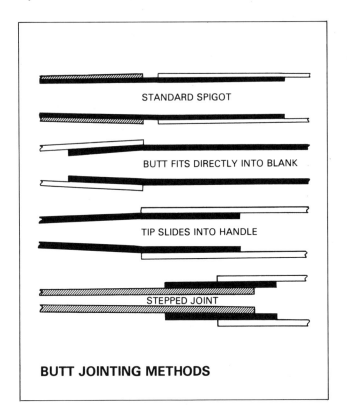

BUTT JOINTING METHODS

Carbonfibre
Carbonfibre is very light, tough, responsive, smooth and lightning fast. The feeling is of an overdrive or turbo-charge boost to the cast. No butt can equal its performance and easy handling. It is expensive; on rods over 12 feet long the butt section costs more than the single-piece tip. These butts are directly responsible for improved tournament records and better fishing. Nobody can afford to make a mistake when buying a carbon handle. Tell the dealer—or better still the blank designer—exactly what kind of rod you need. Buy a matched butt, blanks and spigot. You should know your ideal rod length before ordering, but if in doubt add an extra six inches on to the handle. Nearly all anglers who switch to carbon benefit from a butt slightly longer than they can handle in glassfibre or aluminium alloy.

Measure spigot overlap before gluing the components. A half inch gap is about right on most blanks.

Boron/carbon butts

In theory, boron filaments should improve even a carbonfibre rod butt. The very few handles available are slimmer than pure carbon, extremely stiff and apparently longer-casting. Exactly why, is difficult to say until more work has been done. In my view the very slimness of the handle contributes a marginal boost to the cast. Prices are horrific even though boron content is quite low.

Joints for single tips and separate butts

Long tips and their butts are jointed according to material, comparative diameters and wall thicknesses, and to some extent to individual preference. As with most aspects of blank/handle selection, take advice before you decide, and do try out the rods which appeal to you. There are several methods of attachment, all of them strong and reliable. Some look crude, others are neat but add both weight and cost. Choose either what is available as standard from the blank manufacturer, or carry out your own modifications. One point for American anglers to consider: despite what some rod companies claim, there is absolutely no reason to condemn a plug spigot or indeed the detachable butt format itself. Buy with confidence.

Coat the spigot with candle wax to prevent the walls rubbing each other away.

An all-carbonfibre surf blank weighing less than 10 ounces. The rod is jointed in the centre with a carbon plug spigot. The method of jointing is perfectly safe.

21

The options: Spigot, either Feralite or plug
Blank slides over butt
Butt pushes into blank
Permanent joint
Stepped joint

Spigots

At its simplest, fitting entails little more than measuring the male and female ends of the spigot to ensure a tight, comfortable fit, then gluing the lower end into the handle.

Clean the inside of blank and butt. Wipe the spigot. A thin layer of grease and dust alter the overlap quite considerably and severely reduce adhesion of Araldite-type glue. Methylated spirit works well enough, but special epoxy adhesive thinners are available. Ajax powder on a damp cloth soon scrubs away stubborn particles.

Slide the spigot into the blank. Normally it is impossible to insert the wrong end. Push firmly and twist gently so that the walls fit closely but without stress. Mark the spigot depth with a grease pencil or chalk. Alternatively, stick on a circle of masking tape.

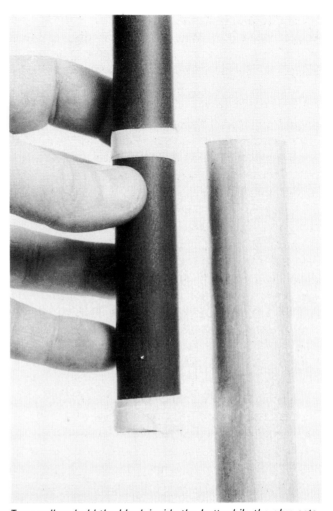

Tape collars hold the blank inside the butt while the glue sets. This is the best way to ensure a straight rod.

Stepped aluminium alloy tubing looks better than a direct fit between substantial butt and slim-line carbonfibre blank.

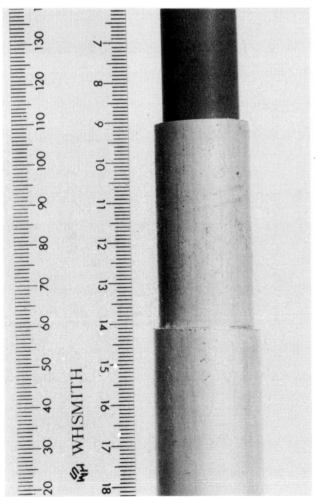

Remove the spigot, then push its other end into the handle. If necessary, rub down the spigot with wet-and-dry paper lubricated with soapy water. A perfect fit is not required. In fact a slightly undersize joint glues up more accurately and securely. You also avoid what is known as hydraulic distortion: soft adhesive in an over-tight joint creates a severe outward radial pressure on the handle walls. In extreme cases the material splits. When you are satisfied with the dry fit, apply glue inside the handle and on the lower section of spigot. Insert the spigot *and remember to leave approximately 0.5 inch between the handle and the blank depth marker.* A gap is essential to accommodate spigot/blank wear.

Where the handle tube diameter is greater than spigot width, build up the gap with string soaked in adhesive or make up a sleeve from segments of a complete ring of suitable glassfibre—from an old blank, for example. String is satisfactory for gaps up to 0.0625 inches. Beyond that, a sleeve of some kind is essential.

Usually a spigot automatically sits square and straight in the butt. Where excessive rubbing down or padding out are involved, slight inaccuracy creeps in. Wrap masking tape (Sellotape will do but tends to melt in contact with adhesive) around the lower end of the spigot until it fits perfectly inside the handle. Slide the spigot home. Mark its exact depth—do not forget to allow for the joint overlap—and build that end exactly to diameter with tape. The dry spigot now sits accurately in the handle, supported top and bottom by tape collars. Attach the blank and check the overall rod straightness. If necessary adjust the tapes accordingly. Slight eccentricity might actually produce a straighter rod.

Apply glue inside the handle and between the tape coils. Slide in the spigot and leave it to set. If padding is necessary, follow the same plan as before with string or sleeves, but this time restrict them to the space between tapes. As long as you use tape no wider than 0.25 inch, joint strength and stability are not affected.

Leave adhesive to cure for at least 24 hours. Keep an eye on the joint until Araldite begins to set. Sometimes the spigot creeps in or out of the blank and must be continually adjusted or held steady with tape or clamp. Check that no glue spreads to the male end of the spigot. If it does, wipe it off with thinners. Finally, rub candlewax on the male spigot. Glassfibre and carbonfibre are slightly self abrasive, and the wax protects one wall of the overlap from the other.

Sliding joints

On rods whose butts slide directly into the tip or vice versa, clean the mating parts, check for security and measure the overlap. Between 4 and 6 inches is adequate on any surf rod. If necessary ease the joint with fine grade abrasive paper and soapy water. How do you find the high spots? Slide the joint together and twist gently. Shiny spots on the withdrawn section indicate excess material. Finally, wax the male side.

Glass into glass, glass into carbon, and carbon into glass are all satisfactory. Glass and carbon blanks are safely inserted into parallel aluminium alloy butt tubes. However, in my experience it is bad practice to plug an aluminium butt into a blank unless the joint is glued permanently. A sliding, detachable alloy handle rapidly wears away the inner blank walls and causes sudden catastrophic failure. On the whole, it is perhaps better to glue down all these joints, in effect making a single-piece rod. Unless there are

Ready for a big pendulum cast. This is the ultimate test of joint strength. Avoid taking short cuts as you build the rod.

transportation and storage problems, that is the method I prefer for all my rods.

Stepped joints

In the case of carbonfibre and some semi-carbon, the external diameter of a blank is far slimmer than the required grade of aluminium alloy handle. A powerful tournament tip slightly more than 0.75 inches diameter might require a 1.125 inch butt, which in 16SWG wall is 1 inch internally. A 0.25 gap is too great to fill with tape. Ordinary jointing methods work but the rod looks silly—a tiny blank sprouting from a damn great chunk of metal.

Try this. Find a piece of 1 inch/10SWG HT15 alloy tube about 8 inches long. The inside diameter is just right to accept the blank. Skim the outer wall by hand or on a lathe until the tube slides into the main handle. Leave a 1–1.5 inch overhang to produce an unobtrusive step, which can be completely hidden by a plastic shoulder collar or even by careful whipping.

When you rub down the smaller tube, make sure it does not stick in the main one while you are testing for diameter. Once aluminium grabs hold of itself, it will not shift. Work on a lathe if possible.

23

Rod Building: Testing and Design

When handle and joint assembly are completed, long-tip blanks follow much the same constructional path as sectional and one-piece blanks. The basic unit is ready for rings, hand grips, reel seat. On well-established designs of rod which the angler knows from experience will suit the way he casts and fishes, there is no need for testing until the final coat of varnish has set. In every other case it pays to break the building process into steps which allow periodic testing and fine-tuning. Stages detailed here incorporate such safeguards. On familiar types of rods, or if you are making a rod for another angler and to his specifications, simply skip over the irrelevant parts. On the other hand, testing takes such little time and effort that many highly competent rod builders still prefer to include it.

STAGE 3: Spine and blank alignment

Because of the way blanks are made, every one has a plane of least resistance running from tip to butt. This is not a weakness in the practical sense; it just means that the blank bends a little more easily in one particular direction. The phenomenon is referred to as spine or bias, and while the effect is greater in some blanks than others there are very few with no spine at all.

The vast majority of blanks are also slightly curved, and the curve itself usually takes the same direction as the spine. Even if a blank appears perfectly straight when held vertical, it assumes a slight downward bias when horizontal because the tip is pulled down by its own weight. Many anglers worry about the curve of a blank and automatically reject those with a detectable bias.

A curve is of no consequence provided it is not a sudden departure from the natural plane of the blank. Twists and bends arising suddenly towards the tip, however, are a danger sign, especially if their onset coincides with a bulge, broken cloth pattern, split, depression or patch of loose filaments. On some blanks made from exotic carbon-based materials, a natural bend is the sign of a superior manufacture. Indeed, when a second-rate manufacturer has trouble making acceptably straight blanks, he may increase the resin content or use an inferior chemical mix. 'Wet' cloth soaked in cheap resin, low mandrel taping pressure and minimum curing are all tricks to improve straightness. They also cut performance, add weight and shorten service life.

Rod makers use the spine and curve of a blank to determine alignment points for rings and reel seat. On high-power surf rods used pendulum style, spine direction must be taken into account because in extreme cases an incorrectly aligned blank twists itself apart, loosens the rings and makes the casting action uncharacteristically harsh. It takes but a few seconds to align a blank for spine and straightness, and in the long run you may avoid ruining your rod.

The classic test is to lean the blank against a wall, butt on the floor, and see where it naturally settles. If the spine is pronounced, the blank rolls over until the inside of the spine curve—the weaker side—faces away from the wall. Mark that plane with a grease pencil or chalk. If the spine is hardly apparent, press on the blank and slowly rotate it by hand. At some stage it will suddenly 'drop' under your fingers. This indicates the spine plane. With practice you can dispense with the wall. Just lean the butt on the ground, bend the tip over and spin the blank until you feel the soft spot.

The relationship of spine to rings varies with blank taper, length and power. Spine may be used to produce an absolutely straight rod: rings are suspended from the outside of the curve, and gravity does the rest. Alternatively, rings may sit on the inside bend, which sometimes makes a rod feel smoother to cast. In flycasting and freshwater fishing where blank power and casting weight are small no damage is likely to result whichever system is used.

Every year I come across more and more high-power surf rods which feel strange in action. Many distort the rings, and some have either cracked the blank walls or snapped altogether. In every case, with the rare exception of a genuinely faulty blank, the cause is misalignment of blank spine. The overwhelming majority of blanks are ringed on the outside of the curve or at right angles to the spine plane. Nine rods out of ten were home-built by surf anglers who forgot to line up the rings with the blank.

During the cast, any blank tries to take the line of least resistance—that is towards the inside of the spine. If rings are set on the opposite side, the blank literally twists itself. In the long run the weaker element fails. Either the rings move around the blank, or the blank walls begin to self-destruct.

My standard practice is now to ring a rod on the inside of the spine curve regardless of the slightly exaggerated bend which may occur when the rod is supported horizontal and rings down. Only fixed spool rods are affected; and with most blanks you must look very hard to see any more distortion than there would have been with the rings on the other side of the spine curve.

Multipliers are no problem since you fish them rings upward. In theory, the blank should then twist when a fish bends it but in practice you do not notice any difference. Fighting pressures are never so vicious as those encountered during the cast.

Long tip blanks with detachable butts and equal-length section rods with stiff butts spliced on may not sit quite straight due to slight imperfections in joint construction. Sight along the rod from butt to tip, and see how the imperfection responds to a slight twist of the spigot. A distinct improvement usually occurs at one particular stage of spigot rotation. Make a chalk dot on each side of the spigot as a reference point. Now carry out the spine test with the sections of blank in precise dot alignment with each other. Mark the spine position on both sections of the rod. Use that line to centre the rings and reel seat. The rod may still look a little bent, but it is safe enough to cast. Complete correction is almost impossible anyway.

STAGE 4: The first test

If my new blank is a prototype, I am so keen to test it that the normal building sequence collapses. With the blank jointed and spined, only 5 minutes' work stands between a fisherman and his first cast with the new toy. Tape on the rings and reel, and off you go. But before you cast the rod—and preferably before you even flex it purposefully—REINFORCE EVERY JOINT WITH A TIGHT WHIPPING. If you don't, the blank walls might well split and render the entire rod useless.

When I'm dealing with prototype blanks in the factory, I rely on a dozen turns of Sellotape or packaging tape strapped around the joints to protect them. My theory is that the rod might snap anyway, being a brand new, untried design. I also want to gain some insight into joint safety. In extreme cases I dispense with tape and deliberately try to split the blank. That is hardly a trick to recommend, though it does prove the point that *no matter how well the rod is made, unprotected joints do split under quite modest pressure*.

Sellotape suits me fine, but I would still suggest you use a proper whipping. Whipping thread is not satisfactory unless impregnated with adhesive. Even tightly bound, the blank might weaken. Nylon monofilament fishing line is far superior because it exerts strong radial support on the blank; 12–15 pound test is excellent. Use modest tension and whip at least 3 inches on each side of

Blank designers often use tape to protect trial rods. It is quick but not always safe. Tough Mylar tape is much better than ordinary Sellotape.

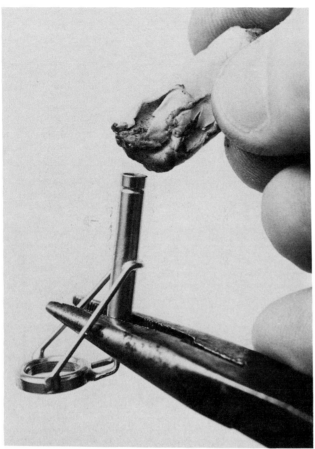

Fix tip rings with hot-melt glue which is easily softened when the ring needs changing. The ring is a Diamite—unquestionably the best choice for hard working surf rods.

every joint, male and female. There is a very slight risk that monofilament could crush thin-walled blanks if the whipping tension becomes excessive. Apart from that, the procedure is safe, quick and easy. Tuck the final turns of line under each other or stick them down with Sellotape.

I fix on my reels with a taped-on Fuji Snaplock, hose clips or strip of rubber whipped over the reel stand. Any method will do provided it holds the reel securely, is instantly adjustable for butt position, and does not crush the blank walls or dig into the surface.

Glue on the tip ring with hot-melt adhesive. Make sure it is exactly in line with the spine—from now on it becomes the reference point for rings and reel seat. Tape on the rings in what seems a reasonable combination and spacing pattern. Sellotape is fine for field testing. Waterproof electrical tape is better if you aim to go fishing rather than just casting. The rod is now quite practical and sound. Two or three of mine never did progress to final building. They have fished and cast beautifully for ten years.

Testing can be as cursory or as exhaustive as you like. If I have experience of the design, a few casts can confirm what I already know about ring spacings, handle length and overall rod length. I

may fiddle around with the rings to check spine angles and see if any minor improvements emerge.

Most fishermen worry about rod testing. They think that without sophisticated equipment and a university qualification, nobody can assess a new rod. Certainly there are some mistakes like not whipping the joints which can ruin a blank. While the very best tournament casters in the world tune their tackle to its limit, even experts manage quite well with less than perfect tackle. A rod two or three inches too short or long will have some effect on performance, but seldom enough to worry one man in a hundred. The best way to test a rod is to try it and see. Fit the thing together, incorporate any useful information gained by experience or gleaned from the angling world, use well-known components . . . and just wave the rod around. Cast it a few times, catch a couple of fish, move the rings up and down, add or subtract a ring, shift the reel seat and feel the various changes in action and power.

There is a lot of nonsense talked about rod design. Fishermen are utterly convinced that within the walls of a rod factory are teams of scientists and technical geniuses who slave over advanced experiments and exotic field test programmes. Rod manufacturers are too clever to dispel the myth, and may even compound it by broadcasting reams of high-flown literature. The poor old fisherman keen to build his own rod feels

A neat tunnel for the line. All good brands of ring will produce an efficient line flow if spaced correctly. These are Daiwa Dynaflo.

he just cannot compete. 'Why', he says, 'I can't do much more than waggle the damn thing around until it feels right.'

In fact, a lot of rod and blank companies, among them the some of the best known in the world, do most of their experimental work by waving rods around. The long-term fortunes of a company reflect the quality of the man in charge of the waggling—known as a designer, development engineer, or design consultant. If his idea of how a good rod should feel coincides with those of the mass market angler, the company is on to a winner. Technical skill and scientific experiment have their place in rod making but mostly involve the chemical engineers who develop the raw materials and the man who works out the shape and size of the blank. After that, the process of 'designing and scientifically field testing' a new model is very much a seat of the pants exercise.

Knowing the truth about so-called scientific rod designing encourages more anglers to go ahead with projects of their own. As a result, more new designs are born in the home workshops of the world than in every tackle factory and custom shop combined. The only restriction is in blank making, which really is beyond the individual angler. However, with so many thousands of blanks now available, the chances are excellent of finding one pretty close to or even exactly right for you.

Consider the argument in terms of rod rings alone. The vast majority of surfcasting and tournament rods, homebuilt and production, are fitted with rings of very few styles, materials and sizes. Almost regardless of their brand and minor variations in design, the number of rings and their diameters fall into two ranges according to reel type. For example, Fuji BNHG series are universally popular for multiplier casting, and BSHG for fixed spool work. Seven or eight rings between 10mm and 30mm is about average for multipliers. Four or five rings grading down from 40 or 50mm suits 99 percent of fixed spool rods. Dynaflo, Seymo, and a dozen other brands follow much the same theme.

Pessimists assume that rings are so special and important that only a few companies have cracked the code, and that only two or three combinations of ring can possibly apply to surfcasting. Anglers who really believe this are neurotic about making a mistake. Under no circumstances will they risk a few test casts. They want to know exactly which rings to buy and where to whip them on—and they want dimensions down to the nearest millimetre.

Optimists conclude that ring sizes and spacing are quite unimportant as long as you choose a set reasonably compatible with the blank and reel.

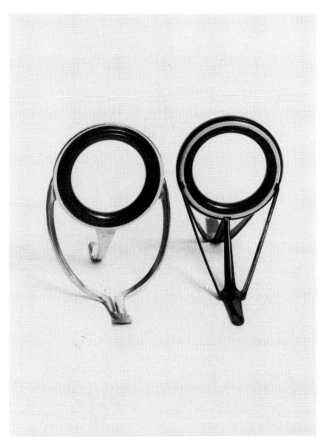

Fuji BNHG and BSHG surfcasting rings. BNHG are used on multiplier rods, BSHG on fixed spool. There is no reason why you cannot change them around.

Fuji lined rings are typical of the modern generation of surfacasting rings. Good casting properties combine with toughness.

A wipe with Ajax scouring cream lifts off dirt and grease. Adhesives and varnish will not stick to a filthy blank.

They argue that, give or take a little, the exact position of the ring is unlikely to destroy casting performance, alter the fishing characteristics of the rod or stress blanks unnecessarily. If this were not so, the fishing industry would need to develop and market thousands more types and sizes of ring. At some stage rods would progress to the point where every blank would have its own special set. The fact that for years nobody has come up with a radically new concept in rings must prove something.

Of course there are differences between rod rings. Changes in pattern do alter the way rods react. My book 'LONG DISTANCE CASTING' covers ring selection in detail for both fishing and casting rods. While I certainly do not go along with some manufacturers' claims about their products, I have found slightly better results with some designs. Overall, given a choice between the two basic philosophies outlined above, I suscribe to the latter. Unless you are making a very advanced rod, time spent worrying about rings and spacings would be better employed elsewhere. However, it is always worth bearing in mind a few cardinal rules.

1) The butt ring's size and distance from the reel are instrumental in controlling line flow. Minimum figures given in the design profile do much to prevent trapped leader knots, high friction and line tangles with fixed spool reels.

2) Set the rings out on the blank to produce a neat tunnel for the line to travel.

3) Try to avoid rings smaller than 10mm inside diameter. They trap weed and foul leader knots.

4) Use a plain tip ring like the Hopkin's and Holloway Diamite. Rings with inserts are notoriously unreliable, and the tip ring is the only one you cannot afford to lose or damage on the beach.

5) Space rings close enough to spread the load evenly over the rod. It is important to prevent localised stress at any point, and especially near the tip of the blank.

6) On the other hand, avoid whipping on too many rings. Extra weight dulls blank reaction and may reduce performance.

The patterns suggested in this book should be satisfactory for the majority of blanks. Anglers with no experience of rod building will find them useful as a starting point. At worst it will be necessary to shift them just a few inches either way, or perhaps add or take a single ring from the set. Confirmation of the ring pattern is smooth casting, plenty of power in the rod, and evenly spread pressure when the rod is held at full curve against a static line.

TESTING FOR ROD LENGTH is based on trial casts and practical fishing. Of the two, casting is far

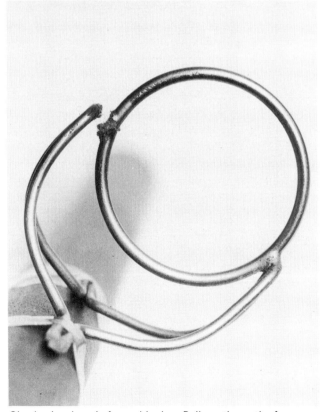

Check wire rings before whipping. Pull gently on the frame brazings. This one looked sound but was completely cracked under the chrome.

28

Spigot reinforcement is essential. Wrap tightly, then glue down and seal the threads.

more important because within reason the length of a rod makes little difference to bite detection, handling and pulling power. Adjustment is usually required only on rods with detachable butts and single-length tips. Most butts are supplied slightly over-long, so you may need to trim back a few inches. You can run quite a few tests without actually cutting the butt. Shift the reel into position and hold the rod a few inches in from the bottom end so that the excess material lies outside your hand spacing. Up to a foot can be accommodated this way. Having found your ideal length, make the cut.

I have already warned about cutting back the tip of a rod. Most rods are better left uncut. Should you feel it necessary to experiment, there is no practical alternative to doing so before rings are finally whipped into place. An inch cut from the tip might destroy the required gap between the tip ring and its neighbour. Sometimes two or three intermediate rings must be moved. Even if tests absorb days of casting and fishing, rely on tape until you are happy with the rod. Trim back inch by inch and make sure you stop in time. The final inch which you didn't know whether to risk is usually the one that wrecks the rod.

Rod building would be easier if every rod did have a set of hard facts and figures to guide its construction. Just accept that nothing is achieved unless you have the confidence to jump in at the deep end. Rod making is a fast-growing offshoot of angling which thrives only because it is a lot easier than it looks. He is a rare fisherman who produces a masterpiece first time; but it is also extremely difficult to make a complete mess.

STAGE 5: Back to square one

Testing a rod inevitably covers the blank with dirt and grease. As soon as you are happy with the tests, measure ring and handle positions, then strip the blank bare, including the joint whippings. Salvage the spine markings and spigot dots, and transfer them to a ring of tape stuck to the blank at some convenient point such as the spigot whipping area or where the reel seat/handgrips will be. Clean the blank with Ajax or methylated spirit, and from now on try to keep it perfect. Once rings and fittings are attached, blanks are almost impossible to treat.

Some blanks are already coated in high-gloss finish and require no more than a wipe down. Blanks with a spiral pattern on the outside and a lustrous finish (actually a layer of resin squeezed from the cloth during manufacture) need no extra protection. Some builders coat them with gloss, most do not bother. All plain blanks need some kind of coat, either varnish or one of the modern two-part epoxy finishes. The decision is whether to coat them now or wait until the rod is finished. For the best possible appearance, do it now. If custom-built looks are of no importance, leave it until the rod is whipped.

High gloss and smooth surface are best achieved by spraying on several coats of thin finish built up layer upon layer. Anglers with access to a spray gun and compressor should have no trouble turning out sparkling blanks. For the rest, dipping is the answer.

To successfully dip-coat a blank you need a length of plastic guttering a little longer than the blank and blocked at both ends to form a tray, a pint of coating and thinners, and a dry room tall enough to permit blanks to hang vertical while drying. First mask off the spigot and seal the ends of blank sections and butt. Pour half an inch of thinned coating into the tray, then drop in the blank and swill it around until every scrap is covered. Pick it up by the tip and hang it upright to dry. Butt downwards is best. Push a tray under the blank to catch the shower of drips. Several thin coats are better than a single dose of syrup.

However you work, make sure the atmosphere is dry, warm and dust-free. Spraying throws off clouds of solvent, some of which are dangerous in confined spaces. Be sure to follow the instructions on the can. Fumes are less of a hazard in dip-coating but soon build up if several rods are treated at once.

I have used all kinds of varnish, high-build specialist rod coats and even paint on surf rod blanks. Yacht varnish and high-build epoxy are best, but without special thinners high-build coat cannot be sprayed or dipped. Be careful with powerful solvents. Many eat into the blank itself. If all else fails, ordinary polyurethane varnish seems as good as anything. Again it depends on whether you have a fetish about appearance, in which case only the expensive products supplied by the custom-building trade will satisfy.

Rod finishing bores me silly. For years I have scoured the market for something you can simply wipe on and polish up. Think of all the time it would save. No dust. No streaks and runs. No waiting for the stuff to harden. Now I've found it: Turtle Wax Formula 3 polymer car wax is what you need, though any equivalent product should be equally good.

Pre-coated and spiral wrap blanks respond beautifully to a few doses of polymer wax. Most of my rods are spiral-wrapped carbonfibre, and these really do shine up after two applications. Besides looking good, the finish is virtually scratch proof. After a bout of heavy fishing, I wash the rods in soapy water and rewax them—blank, whippings and rings. Polymer wax builds into a perfect armour. If anything, rods look better with age, which is more than can be said for those coated in varnish or some of the new specialist rod coatings. Unfortunately, Turtle Wax Formula 3 will not generate a high gloss on plain, sanded blanks. It does, however, build into a smooth, totally protective matt finish.

Rod Building: Handles and Reel Fittings

STAGE 6 — Finishing the butt

Reel seat position is determined by the length and power of the rod, casting style and personal preference. Muscle power, blank stiffness and casting weight are the limiting factors. Adequate leverage is essential; on the other hand, an excessively high reel position reduces tip speed.

Rods in the 11–12 foot range cast pendulum or overhead style usually hit peak performance with a reel set some 28–32 inches from the butt cap. On a general-purpose rod to be used with fixed spools and multiplier reels and 5–6 ounce sinkers, those figures accommodate the vast majority of anglers. If in doubt, bias your decision towards the 32 inch mark. A few inches of excess handle are better than strained muscles and poor casts.

Varying sinker weights demand some leeway in the handle grips anyway: the bigger the weight, the wider the hand spacing should be. A 32 inch butt held 3–4 inches inside the limit provides a 28–29 inch leverage base for casting 5 ounces; the redundant 3–4 inches lying beyond the left hand make no difference to control and balance. When you cast 6 ounces on the rod, shift your left hand to the end of the grip and bring the extra leverage into play.

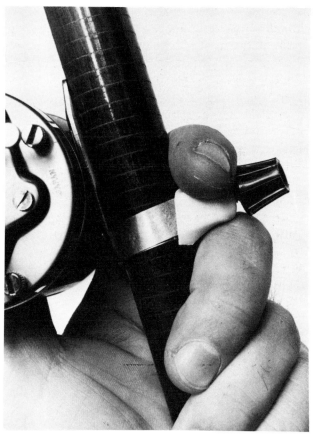

Reel clips are available for butts up to 1.125 inches diameter. If you use the clip as a trigger, wrap soft padding around the steel.

Some minor variations in reel seat position are inevitable if you are particularly long or short in the arm, so it pays to err on the long side rather than splice on an extra butt piece at a later stage. If the butt proves excessively long, trim it back with a hacksaw.

Popular reel seats: Screw winch fitting
　　　　　　　　　　Hosepipe clips
　　　　　　　　　　Reel saddle
　　　　　　　　　　Snaplock
　　　　　　　　　　Rubber strip

Fuji FPS carbon fibre/stainless steel reel seat.

31

The saddle is a quick, cheap method of holding a reel on a parallel butt.

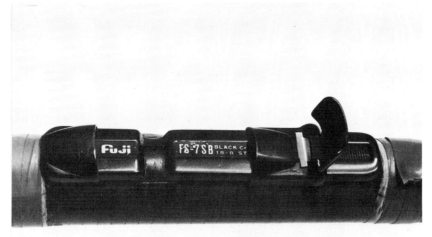

Fuji Snaplock taped to the blank for trial casts. The seat is versatile but none too reliable.

Ordinary hosepipe clips are strong and secure. Trouble is they look horrible and soon corrode.

Screw winch fittings

Tubular seats with sliding collar and locking threads are probably the most secure reel attachment. Modern lightweight fittings like the Fuji FPS stainless steel/plastic seat are reliable, tough and, by virtue of the many sizes in the range, compatible with a vast array of blanks and butts. Any blank with a diameter up to 30mm is a potential candidate for a screw winch fitting; and unless there is an important reason not to fit one, most home-builders are advised to look no farther. Other models besides the Fuji exist, and some of the old-style brass ones are much stronger. However, they are also very heavy and never so versatile. Lightweight aluminium alloy seats are best avoided since the metal crumbles to powder through saltwater corrosion. Choose a seat which matches the diameter of the rod butt, and simply glue it in place with Araldite or another brand of epoxy adhesive.

A limited amount of packing can be incorporated using the same principles described for spigots and butts. Some plastic can be reamed from inside the seat tube, but this is better to avoid if possible. Fuji FPS seats are made in 2mm increments, so there is seldom need to open up a slightly too small model. Which way around should the seat be? Most anglers prefer the threaded side of the tube between reel and butt ring. That way you hold the handgrip not bare threads.

Hosepipe and other clips

Versatility of design is an essential ingredient of rod building. Screw winch fittings are good looking and secure, so they appeal to the practical and aesthetic nature of fishermen. However, the option to move a reel up and down the handle at will is a powerful ally for advanced casters. Fine tuning is impossible with a permanent reel fitting because once the tubular base of the seat is glued down, only a hacksaw or chisel can shift it.

Parallel or slow tapering butts left bare or covered in plastic shrink tube allow free reign for reel adjustment. A stainless steel clip each side of the reel affords an excellent alternative to the traditional seat.

Some tackle manufacturers produce special reel clips with a threaded adjustment knob in sizes to suit butts between 1 and 1.125 inches diameter. As an alternative, screw-slot clips originally meant for hosepipes and automobile cooling systems work just as well, although they do not look as nice and will corrode in time.

Reel saddles

Security saddles supplied with Penn and similar multiplier reels are a viable alternative to a pair of separate clips. Penn saddles are particularly versatile, and if necessary the threaded screws and base can be adapted to fit very large diameter butts. In standard form they suit most butts up to 1.125 inches. Newell clips are very neat and secure but are sometimes too small to clip on aluminium alloy tubes. The small 220F reel is restricted to barely an inch. Some limited adjustment is possible, but full-scale alterations entail machining away the lugs on the base of the reel stand. This is sometimes necessary if you want to attach a small Newell to a large screw reel seat.

Snaplock fittings

Fuji's Snaplock fitting looks like a zip fastener strapped or whipped to the top of the handle. It is also available in tubular form. The fitting works in a similar manner to a traditional screw seat but relies on a clip and corrugated track rather than a sliding collar and thread.

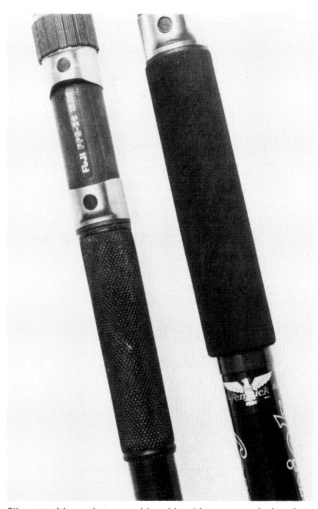

File-cut rubber grips are cold and hard but economical and reliable. Hypalon is expensive and a little more difficult to fit. It is very soft and comfortable, and it looks better.

For lightweight surfcasting and experimental work a Snaplock has much to commend it. Unfortunately, it is unreliable and too weak to handle prolonged casting and fishing pressures in the 6 ounce-plus sinker weight range. Either the whole fitting disintegrates or the security clip skids under load. Loose clips can be repaired but will soon fail again.

In view of their flimsy nature, Fuji Snaplocks are better whipped or taped to the handle. The tubular version can be cut away cleanly, but still leaves an unsightly gap in the blank. Plain Snaplocks combine neatly with a pair of hosepipe clips for use on parallel plain butts, or may be pop-rivetted to aluminium alloy tubes. You should use three rivets, one at each of the normal whipping positions. Some electrolytic damage will inevitably occur, mostly to the rivets themselves.

Rubber strip and sticky tape
Clips and Snaplocks are best used with multiplier reels. Screw seats cannot be moved. So what is the solution for fixed spool casters who want an adjustable reel seat? Try binding the reel stand to the butt with an 18 inch strip of 0.5 inch wide rubber cut from an old tyre. Bind the rubber tightly around the two, and tuck the last 3 or 4 coils around and under each other. Electrician's tape works equally well but is less easily stripped off and re-applied.

Sliding and double seats
A low-set multiplier reel controlled with the left hand makes life much easier on long pendulum and South African-style beach rods. The reel sits about 9 inches from the butt cap. Some anglers find it easy to wind in line and fight a heavy fish. Others wilt under the strain imposed by the reel position.

There are two neat answers. Either use a sliding reel seat—such as clips—or a pair of fixed seats, one high for retrieving, the other glued in casting position. Clips are certainly strong enough for the job, but do require continual opening and closing. There is also an excellent chance that you will drop your reel in the sand. The same drawbacks occur with double Fuji Snaplocks and screw winch fittings, but you soon learn to change the reel position in an instant. If you prefer, use the various fittings in combination. A high-positioned screw seat matches neatly to a pair of stainless steel clips at the bottom of the handle.

A number of special sliding seats have come and gone, and there is currently no specific model available to surf fishermen. However, an ordinary

FPS seat or tubular Snaplock can soon be adapted. The Snaplock is adapted by slitting it from end to end on the reverse face, then attaching it to the rod with a pair of clips. Provided the butt is smooth and almost parallel, devoid of grips and protected from scratching, the system works very well indeed.

An extension butt plugged into the main butt does much the same job as a sliding seat. After the cast, the reel fitting is raised high enough to permit easier retrieve and better leverage. The only drawback is that the rod may be too long and imbalanced for hand-held fishing. It works fine in a rod rest.

Hand grips
Traditional rod builders used cork handles. Tubular sections glued into position, sanded and filled produce a superior rod butt which is warm and comfortable. Of all the materials available, cork looks somehow right for a quality fishing rod.

Good corks are scarce and expensive, especially in the larger sizes. It takes time to assemble and finish the sections, and for best results there is no real alternative to spinning the butt on a lathe. Because surf fishermen generally are more interested in a rod's performance than in its

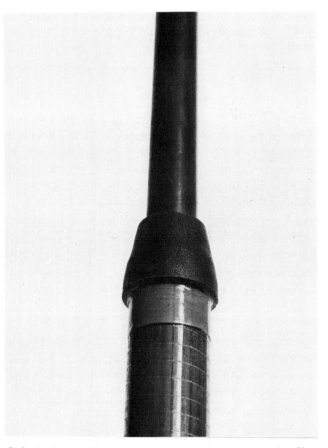

Soft plastic shoulder cap covers the step between a carbonfibre butt and its spigot. You can make your own from rubber or plastic bungs.

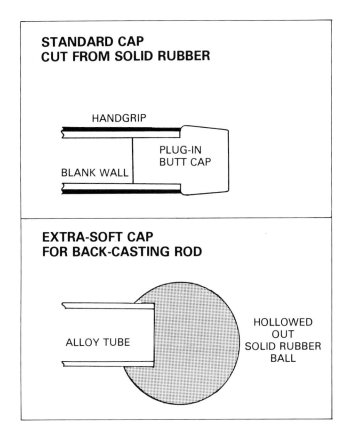

STANDARD CAP
CUT FROM SOLID RUBBER

HANDGRIP

PLUG-IN
BUTT CAP

BLANK WALL

EXTRA-SOFT CAP
FOR BACK-CASTING ROD

ALLOY TUBE

HOLLOWED
OUT
SOLID RUBBER
BALL

appearance, corks have given ground to synthetic materials. Instead of a single-piece handle running the full length of the butt, we now use three handgrips: one at the butt and one each side of the reel seat.

Hypalon and rubber grips are just as effective as cork. Hypalon is a semi-spongy material, reasonably warm and non-slip under the coldest, wettest hands. It is produced in a wide range of diameters, lengths and wall thicknesses, and as far as possible you should choose grips which require little or no alteration. Hypalon is quite difficult to shape by hand. Very careful cutting with an extremely sharp blade followed by rubbing with coarse wet-and-dry paper lubricated with water creates a reasonably good finish. Specialist professional builders and rod factories use power grinders with profiled wheels which cut an exact handle contour. Even then it is a skilled job to turn out perfect grips.

Hypalon's wall thickness is a potential disadvantage. The sponge cannot tolerate a wall less than 0.125 inches thick. A 1 inch diameter butt encased in Hypalon thus expands by at least 0.25 inches. Handles which are much thicker than 1.25 inches are so difficult to grip that fishermen with small hands are unable to hold down a multiplier spool for hard casting. Many of today's powerful surf blanks sport handles over 1.125 inches thick in bare form, so Hypalon is totally unsuitable unless you have hands like a gorilla's.

Thin-walled plastic and rubber sleeves are much more accommodating, but are cold, unappealing and often slippery. However they are used on vast numbers of surf rods, home-built and mass produced simply because there is no acceptable alternative.

Choose whichever grip you prefer. Both offer excellent performance, but Hypalon has the edge in appearance and comfort. The ideal grip is one that slides on to the butt and holds its position by elasticity. If the hole in the grip is between 0.125 and 0.25 inches less than the butt diameter, the tube should slide easily into place and require no glue. Rubber and Hypalon slide more easily if you lubricate the inside of the grip and the walls of the butt with plain water. Soapy water never seems to dry out afterwards and the grip skids under your hand during a hard cast. If a sleeve is difficult to apply, shunt it down the butt with a piece of alloy or hard plastic tube.

Tape, cord and shrink tube
Cork composites consist of slivers of cork or ground particles held together in a resin or rubber matrix. Sheets and tapes are available and both may be cut, spiralled around the butt and glued

Butt caps are more than decoration. Sharp ends of carbonfibre and glassfibre are dangerous.

35

into place. Start and finish of the spiral are best reinforced and protected by whippings or plastic collars, otherwise the tape peels off within a few weeks. Cork composites have most of the advantages of pure cork and are less likely to inflate the butt diameter beyond practical limits. Araldite and Evostik contact adhesive are suitable for bonding cork to alloy, glassfibre and carbonfibre butts.

Rubber, leather and nylon tapes are also used on surfcasting rods. Some are self-adhesive, while others require Araldite or Evostik. Test a small piece of the tape beforehand: some plastics are eaten away by Evostik solvent. As with cork tape, it pays to whip or seal the ends of the spiral. Cord handles are assembled in the same manner. You do not see them around much these days, but some of the old-timers still insist that whipcord is the best handle covering of all.

Plastic shrink tube makes a serviceable butt covering. Many anglers apply it to alloy, glassfibre or carbonfibre butts before adding Hypalon grips or rubber sleeves. Cut the shrink tube 6 inches over-length, slide it on to the butt and warm it over a gas flame or in front of an electric radiant bar. The tube will shrink tightly against the handle, after which you should trim the ends. Spare plastic at the butt cap end can be tucked inside instead of being cut off.

Sometimes it is impossible to make the shrink tube grip the butt. The underlying alloy or blank is cold enough to repel the shrink tube. The plastic seems to tighten down, but it cannot compress through the final millimetre to the blank wall. Warm the butt before sliding on the tube. In rod factories it is common practice to heat the butt rather than the shrink tube. You can do that at home with alloy butts, but I would not recommend it for glass and carbon. Resins used in their construction are susceptible to heat, so you could easily ruin the blank.

Shrink tube lies firm under rubber sleeves and Hypalon grips but will not support a screw winch fitting. Glue that to the bare butt, then slide on two sections of shrink tube, one from each end. Push an inch or so of excess tube over the reel seat, shrink the plastic, then trim back. Some anglers leave a slight overhang permanently over the ends of the reel seat to prevent water creeping between the tube and the underlying butt. This is particularly important with alloy tubes. Six months of hard fishing will allow saltwater to creep inside and rot the butt to powder.

Butt caps and shoulder collars
Butt caps are essential. They look neat, but that is not the main reason to include them on a surf rod. Safety heads the list. An uncapped butt is potentially dangerous if line snaps in mid-cast. Casting force drives the end of the handle into your chest or stomach. Bare alloy, glass and carbon can cut deeply. Glass and carbon may leave behind sharp splinters which are extremely difficult to detect and remove. Back-casters are unlikely to make two casts without a soft, broad cap. During the cast, the butt rides on the hip bone or against your stomach. The first cast hurts so much that you will not be tempted to cast again without adequate protection. There are dozens of kinds of rubber butt caps on sale. Slide one on before you carry out even the initial casting tests on a new blank.

Shoulder collars are either cosmetic or glued in position to stop saltwater running down the upper end of an alloy butt. Either buy one from your tackle dealer or cut your own from a suitable tube of plastic or rubber. I have used cut-down 35mm film containers on several rods. They look quite neat. As a matter of fact, they make nice butt caps as well—a little on the hard side, but long-lasting and safe enough. Araldite holds them in place if the blank is too small for a compression fit.

Rod Building: Rings and Finishing

With the butt completed, ring sizes and spacings established, and spine determined, you are within a few hours of completing a new surf rod. The next stages are so easy that you tend to rush, which makes little difference to the performance and reliability of the rod, but does mar its appearance. Dust, finger prints, lumps and whiskers in the final coating spoil an otherwise perfect rod. Hastily written lettering never looks as good as careful script; and most of us do better with Letraset or a transfer anyway.

Perhaps the biggest failing is to apply more adhesive or coating before the previous layer is fully hardened. Traditional varnishes are notoriously slow to toughen and it is a natural reaction to apply the top coat a little too soon. The result is disaster. For this reason alone you may find modern fast-curing epoxy and polymer coats a much better alternative. Using the very best of them, it is possible to build a rod one day and fish with it the next.

STAGE 7: Whipping on the rings

Whipping is both traditional and effective. In the rush to simplify and hasten rod building, rod manufacturers have tested nylon collars, shrink-tube sleeves and adhesive tapes which in theory should be an improvement on normal thread. Some work fairly well, but none looks as good. Some require special equipment to apply and harden. In time, someone is bound to develop a better alternative, but for now it is the best choice for home-built and custom-made rod building. Surf rod builders should be even more sceptical about so-called 'improved' ring attachment systems. They have more to lose than freshwater and fly fishermen simply because a surfcaster inflicts far more punishment on the rod. Rings are always under attack, and you cannot afford to make any compromises.

Selecting whipping thread

Gudebrod NCP thread is an excellent choice. Available in a wide range of colours, plain and patterned, and in lengths and diameters to suit every kind of rod, Gudebrod is the tackle industry's choice. Very few high-quality rod makers use anything else. The closest rival is Talbot nylon thread available in Britain from a limited number of retail outlets.

Gudebrod NCP is smooth, colour-fast, compatible with most adhesives and rod coatings, and extremely tough. It costs more than inferior brands of thread, but in the long run it is much cheaper. Poor quality materials are covered in loose ends and bristles which become apparent after the first layer of adhesive or varnish. It is then too late to rectify your mistake without stripping off the rings and starting again. Often the blank itself must be cleaned and re-finished. Colours fade or, worse still, discolour when you brush on the finishing coat. Most have to be sealed and doped for security—a stage which can successfully be omitted with Gudebrod and modern synthetic coatings.

As a rule, medium-weight thread is excellent for surf rods. 50 metres is enough for most blanks, although it pays to buy 1 ounce spools instead. Each contains enough to whip two or three surf rods, with plenty left over for repairs later on.

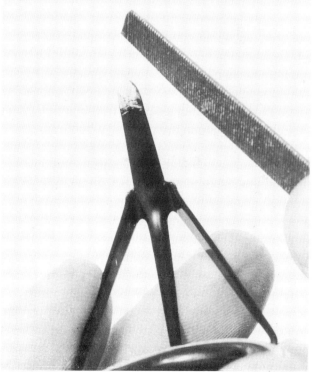

File down the end of the ring feet so that thread climbs easily from the blank.

When you buy thread, bear in mind that reinforcement whippings on spigots and other joints swallow up more than the rings combined; 50 metres is cutting it fine on a 14 foot back cast rod with substantial joint overlaps.

In general, lightweight thread produces a neater finish, although this should be balanced against the slowness of laying on so many coils. Where an absolutely perfect custom-finish is necessary, use thin thread and take great pains to align each coil against each other. Most surf men opt for the medium weight thread, which looks very good but takes less time to apply. The thickest is acceptably tough, very quick to wind on, but always looks coarse. Whipping pressure comes into it as well: thin and thick threads are less controllable than medium-weight Gudebrod, which seems to automatically flow on to produce the correct tension. It also rolls neatly up from the bare blank to the ring foot. Thick thread is likely to produce a nasty gap at the blank/ring junction.

Ring whipping tools
Like thousands of fishermen who make a few rods for their own use, I could get by with a pair of scissors and a roll of Sellotape. Results are perfectly acceptable, and I doubt if anyone could tell exactly how the whipping was produced. The limiting factor is time. While a fisherman is quite content to spend all evening whipping on one set of rings, the semi-professional rod builder cannot afford such luxury. Time means money. He prefers to invest in extra equipment which substantially cuts the labour involved.

A simple whipping frame like the one illustrated is easy to make and operate. The 'V' frame holds a blank steady and allows free rotation; the line holder feeds thread at the correct tension and angle. On my gadget, whipping thread is stored on a multiplier reel. Using the reel's very accurate drag system, I dial in any pressure I need. Other whipping frames, home-made and commercially manufactured, usually rely on a simple tensioning attachment that feeds thread directly from its spool. They work well enough; but by clipping on a reel instead you save time and trouble making a spool holder/tensioner, and you gain sensitivity and control. Just wind the thread on to your ordinary fishing multiplier.

Full-length frames are popular but are far from essential. A frame 12 inches wide supports most blanks with ease. To work right at the blank tip, I

An efficient wrapping frame for surf rods. Thread is carried on the reel spool and fed off under precise drag tension.

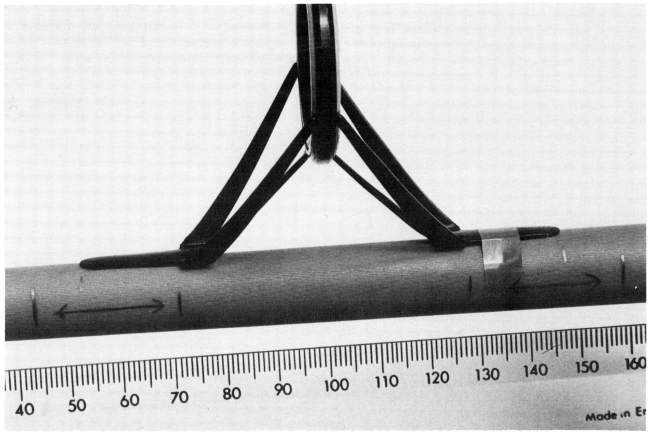

Measure the length of the whipping before you begin. These marks are exaggerated for clarity. A very light pencil line will do.

slide a pile of books or a chunk of wood under the butt for extra balance and control. Anyone can knock together a simple frame from scrap pieces of wood nailed together; or you can make a beautifully finished frame with all the gadgets. Exotic whipping frames are built on the lathe principle with a motorised headstock and speed controller. If speed is essential, the investment is worthwhile. A friend of mine who builds rods commercially reckons that a skilled operator can whip a surf blank, tip to butt including reinforcements, in five minutes on a motorised frame. Mass-produced rods are whipped on much the same principle in two or three minutes, but the standard falls short of that demanded by the custom-rod trade.

A warm, dry and dust free room is essential for varnishing. Thin coats built up one after another are the best. You cannot afford to risk a sudden dust storm—a heated box with air filters offers worthwhile advantages if you build enough rods to justify the outlay. Today's high-build rod coats are best applied to a continuously spinning blank, otherwise the coat sags in one plane. A motorised frame turning three or four times a minute ensures first class results. The home-builders only option is to turn the blank by hand. No trouble with one rod; but you would find half a dozen rods impossible to manage without semi-automated machinery of some kind.

Checking and preparing the rings

Fuji and Dynaflow rod rings, first choice of most discerning anglers, are fairly tough and well made. Chances of their being broken before fitting are slim, but it pays to be sure. Check the frame and its spot-welds, and the security of the linings. Hardchromed wire rings are notoriously weak: until saltwater corrosion highlights the fault with a layer of rust, small cracks in the soldered frame may be almost impossible to spot unless you GENTLY apply pressure to the frame joints. A surprising number of newly-whipped rings do turn out to be faulty.

The ends of ring feet are either ragged, or else the metal is a little too thick for the whipping thread to climb. Every ring should be carefully examined and filed down if necessary. A sharp edge promotes neat whipping but also risks digging into the blank. Some compromise is necessary. Fuji and Dynaflo are nicely shaped in the factory and only the bigger rings require trimming.

Positioning the rings

Ring position has already been determined and tested. Strap one end of the ring foot to the blank, and be sure that the position is correct radially as well—to match the spine curve. Exact alignment in this plane is almost impossible to maintain throughout the whipping process, but do not let the ring slip too far. Sighting down the blank is the best way to check the relationship of the rings to

39

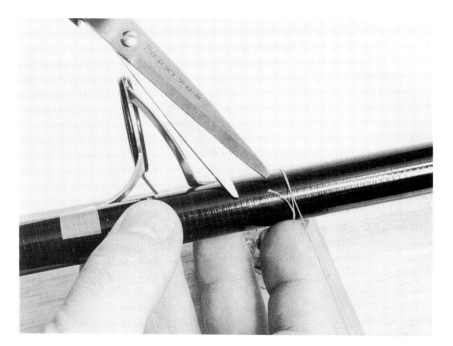

Whipping 1. Wrap the end of the thread around the blank and trap it under the next three or four coils.

Whipping 2. Set the thread tension modestly high, then start to build up the whipping. Lay the thread as neat as possible.

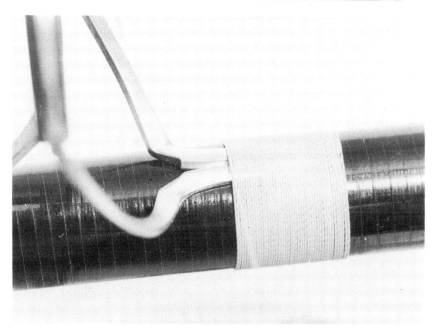

Whipping 3. Work smoothly up the ring foot until the whipping is within a few wraps of its full length.

Whipping 4. *Insert a loop of nylon and continue to whip to full length.*

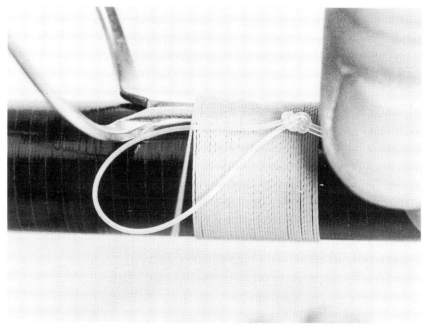

Whipping 5. *Cut the thread, feed the end through the nylon loop, then pull it through.*

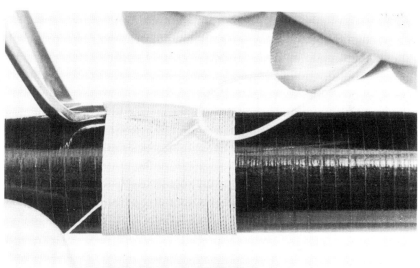

Whipping 6. *Trim the thread, but do not try for a perfect cut at this stage.*

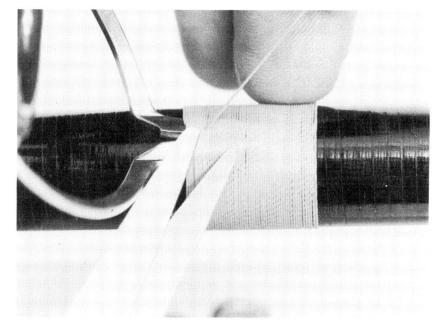

41

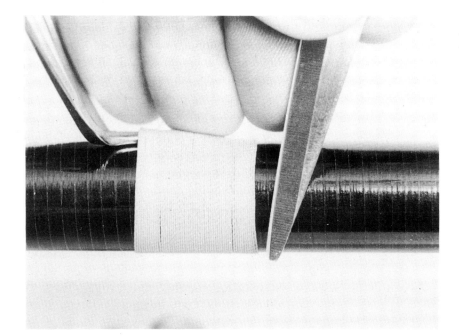

Whipping 7. Square up the ends of the whipping with a knife blade or scissors.

Whipping 8. Smooth the whipping thread to remove gaps. Any smooth metal or hard plastic rod will do. This is the point from an arrow shaft.

Whipping 9. Trim the loose end of thread by cutting down between two coils.

each other, and it helps if you use the tip ring as a baseline. The ring itself should be glued into place and in line with the blank spine. Use hot-melt adhesive, not Araldite. Tip rings usually have to be changed several times during a rod's life.

Use a ruler and soft pencil to mark out the start and finish of each whipping. With experience you can guess the spacings, but it never does any harm to include a pencil line; there is nothing worse than a rod with uneven whippings. No precise formula exists or is necessary to determine whipping length. Design an overlay which matches the ring and blank. As a general rule, the bigger the ring and thicker the blank, the longer the whipping should be.

The patch of Sellotape used to hold a ring is usually removed before the second side of the whipping is applied. However, it is permissible to use a tiny sliver of tape on both sides of the ring to bridge the blank/ring foot step. Whipping thread climbs smoothly up the tape to produce a neat finish.

Marking out the blank is even more important if you prefer to add a tipping of contrasting colour thread to the main whipping. The tipping length itself should be measured. Either make a second pencil line on the blank, or count the number of turns of thread. It is quicker to count and probably more accurate as well.

Length of spigot reinforcements should also be marked out for both safety and neatness. Whipping should extend to or a little beyond spigot depth. On a long joint, you can divide the whipping into several rings. If tippings or patterns are required, carefully mark all the dimensions directly on the blank.

Complex patterns—starbursts, tartan and even signatures—are beyond the scope of this book. For precise details and designs, refer to books on custom building. Some manufacturers produce excellent leaflets. Gudebrod provide full details and comprehensive instructions; Fenwick Wood-stream's blank catalogue sometimes features interesting work.

Underwhipping is a layer of thread applied across the ring position before the ring itself is whipped on. It is both decorative and protective. If you like the effect, go ahead. An underwhipping will stop ring feet from digging into a blank, but should not be used to counteract ring twist unless you are sure of the cause. Some rings do loosen and shift around the blank. It is a natural effect of the ring size and height. An underwhipping and a coat of glue between base threads and ring feet are a satisfactory cure.

The risk is that glue and underwhipping are used to counteract spine misalignment or severe rod torsion from the caster's faulty technique. In both cases a glued-down ring merely transfers the force to the blank, and may ruin it in time. Though underwhips look nice on any custom-finished surf rod, they are technically essential on very few.

Whipping the ring
Two methods are popular in the home-build, custom rod and manufacturing worlds. The easiest way is to tie off each whipping in turn. But when the blank is spun on a frame, motorised or not, a single continuous stream of thread can be wound from tip to butt. Using this technique, a rod can be whipped in a matter of minutes; given good adhesives and coatings, the whippings are just as strong and secure as any other.

Tied-off whippings
The photographs are self-explanatory. Work carefully between the pencil lines to ensure even-length whippings that match the ring size. Use moderate tension, and keep your fingers clean if you feed thread by hand. A piece of 10–15 pound test nylon is just right to pull the last coils of thread under one another. Do not worry about trimming the loose ends at this stage. After one side of each whipping has been done, re-align the rings before finishing the job.

Continuous whippings
Using a proper whipping frame and fully supported blank, start at one end of the blank and whip each spigot reinforcement and ring foot in turn. Unless you use a proper lathe device it is a little easier to begin at the tip and work down. Remember: there are no individual tie-off points other than the very top and bottom of the rod. They are formed by tucking under with the same pull-through nylon loop used in the other technique. Try to maintain even tension on the thread, and work fairly slowly to prevent coils building up on themselves or creeping apart. Although you whip up one ring foot and down the other (usually thought bad practice by the old school of rod builders), rings are held securely and neatly.

There is no reason why continuous-thread whippings cannot be tipped with a contrasting colour applied in individually tied sections or run continuously along the blank. However, it takes considerably experience to do this without disturbing the original layers of thread. How do they do it in rod factories? Usually they don't—tippings are painted on with deeply pigmented dyes. Patterns and fancy whippings have to be applied individually no matter how carefully you work. They are totally incompatible with one-piece machine whipping technique. Try thinking your way through a tartan while the blank spins at 100 revolutions a minute!

Tidying up the whippings
Align side rings with the tip ring. With care, you can wriggle frames into exact position. Should any be fixed too tightly to the blank by thread tension, undo one side of the whipping and then make the necessary adjustment.

white thread retains its sparkle. However, there is no harm in applying a dose of colour preservative if you like. It is far more important to stick the threads to each other and to the blank.

Whipping is incomplete until throughly impregnated with adhesive. Plain varnish is ineffective. Use either glue plus varnish, or a proper finishing adhesive like two-part epoxy— 'Hi-Bild' rod finish as it is commercially labelled. Buy a suitable product and use it according to the maker's directions. Some are single-coat, others are built up from an initial thin, highly penetrative coat to a final thick shell.

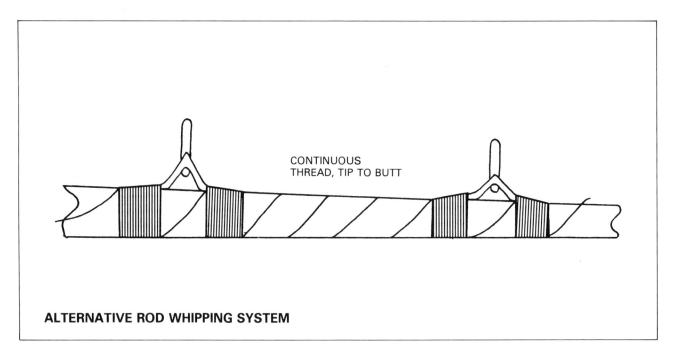

CONTINUOUS THREAD, TIP TO BUTT

ALTERNATIVE ROD WHIPPING SYSTEM

Square off the front and back of each whipping with the edge of a knife blade so that the coils run straight around the blank rather than elliptically. Notice how coils of thread in the main body of whipping are still a little uneven no matter how much care you took. Even them up by rubbing flat with a smooth steel, brass or hard plastic rod about 0.125 inches diameter. Rub from the end of each whipping to its centre; that way you will not open up the threads at the far end of each stroke. Afterwards, trim the loose ends of individually tied-off sections. Rather than use scissors, slide a sharp knife or razor blade between two coils of thread so that the spare end is cut at the base of the whipping, and not on top. Continuous-thread whippings can be straightened and flattened at this stage, but of course you must not trim them yet.

Sealing and gluing
There is really no need to dope-tighten or colour-preserve Gudebrod NCP thread. Given a suitable finish coat—*not* ordinary varnish—even

High-build rod coatings are very expensive in Britain. Most are imported from America, home of custom building. Fanatics prefer to pay the going rate rather than settle for second-rate materials, but if you are more interested in a quick, effective method of finishing your whippings, try a clear epoxy adhesive or even Araldite. I have tested several readily available, cheap brands from Woolworth, Halfords and do-it-yourself shops and found them all acceptable.

Use rapid setting or standard type depending on how long you can afford to wait for the rod to dry. Although the slow-curing mixture finally produces a slightly superior finish, I particularly value the rapid varieties. Rod whippings coated in the morning are hard enough for light duty by afternoon. Application is essentially the same whichever you choose; only the inter-coat drying time differs. Never risk applying a second coat until the first is thoroughly set. Otherwise they tend to fuse together, bubble and finally lift off.

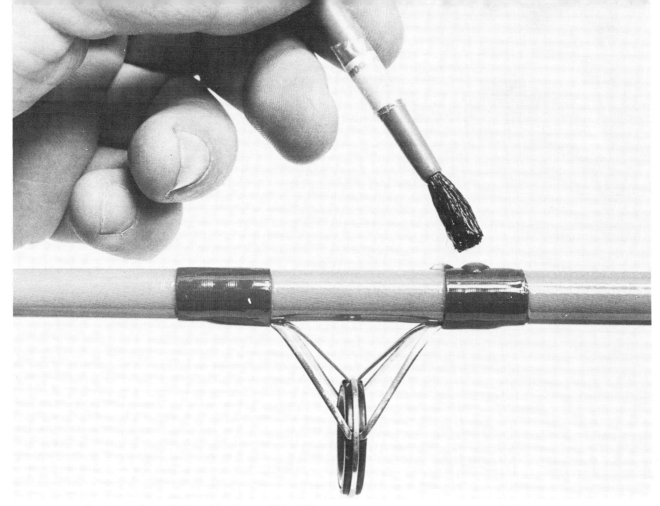

Hi-Bild custom finish is easily applied to whippings and blank. Because it dries slowly, the coating must be kept on the move to prevent drips and lumps. Rotate the rod two or three times a minute.

Araldite coating method

Whippings should be rubbed smooth and trimmed if necessary. Fill a cup with boiling water, and immerse the two tubes of adhesive—hardener and resin. When they are really hot, squeeze out measured amounts into a warm container—I use a 35mm film can—and mix thoroughly but gently to avoid excessive bubbling. The adhesive is runny enough to be brushed on to the thread. Apply a thin coat well rubbed in. Allow it to set hard.

After a couple of hours, mix a second dose of Araldite and brush it on evenly but fairly thick. The first coat should have glued down and sealed the threads, so this time the resin builds a thick layer over the whipping. Support the rod horizontally, and slowly rotate the blank until the Araldite has gelled enough to defy gravity.

Minor air bubbles are destroyed by passing the whipping high over a gas flame whilst slowly turning the blank. Clean brushes and fresh Araldite are reasonably good insurance against lumps and whiskers; you will discover that the coating dries almost transparent. While I would not recommend Araldite as the perfect custom-finish, it is more than adequate for general-purpose surf rods. White thread tends to discolour a little, so it is better to use a fairly dark, well saturated colour instead. Light yellow and blue are about the practical limit.

Most epoxy adhesives work well enough. Some are available with thinners which aids the initial whipping saturation, essential for firm adhesion and smooth foundation. Check before mixing solvents with different brands of glue. Some combinations are effective; others destroy the adhesive properties and cause the resin to bubble and set unevenly.

Varnish and continuous-thread finishes

In my opinion oil-based and polyurethane varnishes are obsolete in rod building. Anglers who still rely on them usually discover that whippings fail to restrain big rings. In fact most surf rods are unstable if the whipping is merely varnished. So even if you insist on the traditional materials, do coat the whippings beforehand with at least one coat of dope or well-thinned epoxy.

There is no alternative to using adhesives on continuously-whipped rods. Brush a coat of Araldite or special rod finish on to the whippings and rub it well in. When the adhesive is absolutely cured—leave it overnight if possible—trim back the ends of each whipping to remove excess thread. Good resin seals the threads to the blank so well that the 'loose' ends of each cut in the thread will not unravel. By trimming the thread very close to and parallel with the body of the whipping, you produce such a neat whipping that

45

without examining the thread under a hand lens nobody can tell which method was used.

Finishing the rest of the rod

Many of the best blanks are pre-coated with gloss finish before they leave the factory. After whippings are coated, a rod is virtually complete. Fastidious anglers will probably run over the whole rod with one last coat of varnish or epoxy-based finish; anglers more interested in casting and fishing will not bother.

Araldite is useless as an overall rod finish. Use varnish or, better still, a specialist two-part coating that builds into a shiny, tough layer around blank and whippings. These one coat high-build resins are easily applied by brush but you *must* keep the rod spinning until the stuff has throughly gelled. If not, the rod literally drips with messy blobs of cured plastic. As most specialist rod finishing products harden relatively slowly—up to 24 hours—it is essential to use a motorised frame.

The saving grace of varnish is that it can be applied very thin, by spraying, dipping or rubbing on with a finger. Several coats spread over ten days eventually produce a mirror-like surface. The trouble is, it soon scratches. At the other extreme, why not coat the blank and whippings with a generous helping of polymer car wax? It takes 2 minutes to protect a rod, and on the right base (see blank preparation section) the results look perfectly all right.

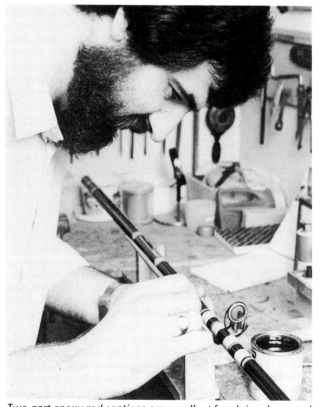

Two-part epoxy rod coatings are excellent for gluing down and finishing the whipping. Araldite adhesive is a quick alternative.

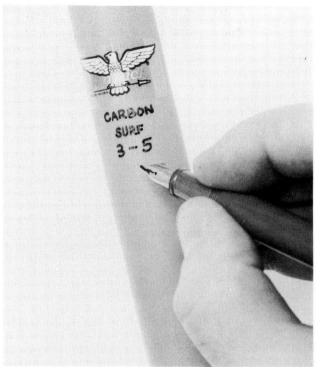

Decals and lettering add that final touch to a new rod. Commercial dry transfers like Letraset are excellent. But with care you can get away with marking ink and pen.

Lettering and transfers

Lettering adds the personal touch to a new rod. Anglers with a steady hand and neat script simply write on the blank with a mapping pen and white ink. (Actually, water-based typewriter correcting fluid is better). The results look most impressive. The rest of us make a rotten job of it. Rub-on commercial lettering like Letraset is so much easier and neater. A variety of type styles and founts are available. Some join up to form italic or copperplate script. The best time to apply lettering is between coats of varnish or before a single high-build layer.

Thin transfers (decals) which you soak in water and float on to the blank are better applied between coats of finish or even on to the bare blank. Thicker self-adhesive decals and stickers should be applied last. Most of them peel off in a few weeks anyway, so it is not worth sealing them in.

Rod bags, tubes and blank plugs

The finest rod can be destroyed by two or three journeys inside or on the top of a car. Just having it stand around at home guarantees dust, scratches and accidental damage. Sew a strong canvas or soft-lined nylon bag for your rod. Better still, make up a tube from plastic drainpipe with wooden end caps. Keep dirt out of the spigots by blocking the open ends with a soft rubber plug. Small details like this preserve your blank for years and prevent cracked rings and loose joints.

Rod Design Profiles

It is impossible to list every available surfcasting blank. These profiles give you an insight into the design of most popular rods for all kinds of fishing and for tournament casting. Armed with this background information, you can go ahead and choose your own specific blank from those stocked by your local dealer or listed in mail order advertisements.

11.5–12.00 FOOT PENDULUM ROD, MULTIPLIER VERSION

Basic construction:
7.75–8.5 foot glassfibre, semi-carbon or carbon tip made up to length with spigot-jointed or permanently attached butt section. Suitable blanks include Conoflex 240T, 100/5 and Cod 5 or 6; Fenwick Surfstik Model 5; Zziplex Dream Machine and semi-carbon range.
Bruce & Walker make a special 8 foot tournament-grade carbon tip to order.

Handle materials:
1 inch/16SWG HT15 aluminium alloy for high reel position.
1.125 inch/16SWG HE30 alloy for low reel position or as an alternative to HT15.
Glassfibre or carbonfibre/alloy laminate.
High performance carbon butt.

Handle assembly:
Plain with sliding clips or rubber grip/fixed screw seat. Optional double seat for casting with reel low.

Rings:
Fuji BNHG, Daiwa Dynaflow or equivalent. 30 mm butt ring spaced at least 36 inches from reel face. 12–16 mm Hopkins and Holloway Diamite tip ring. Fill the blank with appropriately matched and spaced rings. 25, 20, 16, 16, 12, and 12 mm would suit most blanks.

Reel spacing:
29–32 inches above butt cap for most anglers.
Alternatively, mount the reel about 6 in from the butt cap and control it with your left hand.

Casting weight:
Optimum performance with 5–6 ounces. Ideal for 150 gm tournament work. Also capable of fishing with up to 8 ounce sinkers. Leader weight 40–50 pounds; main line 10–30 pounds.

Fixed spool version:
Same basic construction. Reel spacing 26–29 inches. BSHG rings. 50 mm butt guide at least 40 in from the face of the reel. 16 mm Diamite tip ring.
40, 30, 25 and 20 mm intermediate rings spaced according to blank length and action.

12–13 FOOT SENSITIVE BEACH ROD FOR MAXIMUM SPORT AND GOOD CASTING

Basic construction:

Two-piece full length blank.
Cheap glassfibre versions based on Sportex or Conoflex range of blanks. Mid-quality rod: Confoflex and Zziplex 3–6 ounce semi-carbon range.
Highest quality all-carbon blanks: Bruce & Walker 12 and 13 foot high-modulus surfcasting blanks.

Handle materials:

Integral with blank except for some Conoflex and Zziplex blanks.

Handle assembly:

Hypalon grips and Fuji FPS carbonfibre/stainless steel screw seat. Optional plain butt with clips.

Rings:

Fuji BNHG, Daiwa Dynaflo or equivalent. 25–30 mm butt ring spaced at least 30 inches from reel face. 12–16 mm Hopkins and Holloway Diamite tip ring. Fill the blank with appropriately matched and spaced rings. (25), 20, 16, 12, 12 and 10 mm would suit most blanks.

Reel spacing:

Reel in high position 26–29 inches from butt cap.
Even the 13 foot rods can be cast without resorting to the low-set reel.

Casting weight:

Optimum performance with 3–5 ounces.
Leader weight 25–40 pounds.
Main line 8–20 pounds.

Fixed spool version:

Same basic construction. Reel spacing is similar 40–50 mm butt guide at least 60 inches from reel. 16 mm tip. 40, 30, 25 and 20 mm intermediate rings spaced according to blank length and action. Lightweight wire rings may be used. BSHG replace BNHG.

13–14.5 FOOT BACK CAST ROD

Blank:

8–8.5 foot very powerful glassfibre or semi-carbon blank with spigot or spliced-in joint. Conoflex Zziplex, North Western and Pateke Morton supply suitable blanks. Fast or medium-fast action is preferred.

Handle materials:

1.25–1.375 inch/16SWG HE30 alloy tube.
More exotic laminated and carbon butts used in tournaments are extremely expensive.

Handle assembly:

Rubber taped or shrink-tube covered butt with reel mounted close to the butt cap. Screw seats, Fuji Snaplocks and tape straps hold the reel.

Rings:

Fuji BSHG 50 mm butt ring at least 72 inches from the reel face. Then 40 mm, 30, 25 and 20 BSHG according to rod length and action. 16 mm Diamite tip ring.

Reel spacing:

Low position only. The vast majority of back cast fishermen use only fixed spool reels.

Casting weight:

Optimum performance with 5–8 ounce sinkers.
Leader weight 45–65 pounds.
Main line 12–30 pounds.

12–13.75 FOOT PENDULUM ROD, MULTIPLIER VERSION

Basic construction: 8.0–8.5 foot glassfibre, semi-carbon or carbon tip made up to length with spigot-jointed or permanently attached butt section. Suitable blanks include Conoflex and Zziplex tournament semi-carbons and Bruce and Walker 13.5 foot all-carbon tournament/surf blank and special butt.

Handle materials: 1.125 inch/16SWG HE30 alloy.
Glassfibre or carbonfibre/alloy laminate.
High performance carbon butt.

Handle assembly: Plain with sliding clips or rubber grip/fixed screw seat. Optional double seat for casting with reel low.
Most anglers would use the low reel position.

Rings: Fuji BNHG, Daiwa Dynaflo or equivalent. 30 mm butt ring spaced at least 40 inches from reel face. 12–16 mm Hopkins and Holloway Diamite tip ring. Fill the blank with appropriately matched and spaced rings. 25, 20, 16, 16, 12, and 12 mm would suit most blanks, but for low reel position extra rings may be necessary.

Reel spacing: Normally cast with reel set 9 inches above the butt cap and controlled by the left hand. Use either double reel seat or extension butt for line retrieve.

Casting weight: Optimum performance with 5–6 ounces. Ideal for 150 gm tournament work. Also capable of fishing with up to 10 ounce sinkers. Leader weight 45–55 pounds; main line 12–35 pounds.

Fixed spool version: Same basic construction. Reel spacing is similar. 50 mm butt ring at least 60 inches from reel. 16 mm tip. 40, 30, 25 and 20 mm intermediate rings spaced according to blank length and action. Fuji BSHG are ideal.

10–10.5 FOOT LONG-RANGE SPINNING ROD

Blank: Two-piece Bruce & Walker Carbon Sea Spinner 10.5 foot. Fenwick Surfstik 2. 'S' glassfibre/carbon butt.

Handle materials: Integral or supplied with blank.

Handle assembly: Hypalon grips and Fuji FPS carbonfibre/stainless steel screw seat. Optional plain butt with clips.

Rings: Fuji BSHG, Daiwa Dynaflo or equivalent. 40 mm butt, then 30, 25, 20 and 16 mm intermediates tipped by 12 mm Fuji or lightweight Diamite. Space according to blank action and length. The same rings can be used with both fixed spool and multiplier in this case.

Reel spacing: Reel in high position 23–26 inches from butt cap.

Casting weight: Optimum performance with 1–4 ounces.
Leader weight 15–25 pounds.
Main line 8–20 pounds.

Reels—Test Before You Buy

High quality surfcasting reels like Penns, Ambassadeurs, DAMs, Mitchells and Daiwas offer a wide range of line capacities, retrieve speeds and casting performance. Chosen to match your casting technique and the basic demands of your local beaches, any of the popular models should provide long service, excellent casting distances and ample power to control heavy fish and tough conditions. Multipliers and fixed spools, their selection and basic tuning are fully discussed in LONG DISTANCE CASTING.

From the keen shore angler's point of view, reel maintenance and modifications are far more important than initial selection. Very often you have little choice in reels anyway. British tournament casters choose between two multipliers—Daiwa Millionaire and ABU Ambassadeur CT. No other mass-production reel is suitable for specialist work of this kind. Sheer casting power is all that counts; it matters little that the two reels in question are slow retrievers, weak geared and unable to hold more than 150 yards of 20 pound-plus line. Where 250 yard competition work and ultra-long range fishing are involved, there really is no alternative. Except in minor details and name, Millionaire and CT Ambassadeurs are virtually the same anyway.

Choice is similarly restricted in high capacity reels that withstand cranking at full power under heavy load. Channel bass, conger eel and rocky beach anglers looking for easy control, adequate casting range and tough, reliable fishing will almost certainly home in on the Penn Magforce range, ABU Striper, 8000C, 9000C and 10000C Ambassadeurs. What else offers built-in casting control, capacity and speed? Not much apart from the old-style Squidders and Surfmasters. They are plain reels without controls, so you are in trouble if you rely on brake blocks or magnets to smooth the cast. The majority of today's surf and beach fishermen would opt to spend extra cash for a reel that eliminates backlash.

Similar restrictions apply to every branch of surfcasting. When you cut through to the bones of reel selection, you find that despite the vast array of models on sale only a few are worth buying, and of those only one or two match up to your personal preferences. Preferences change of course; new reels arrive on the market every year. Even so, at any given time an experienced surf angler will settle for only a handful of models. You can't wean him away from them, come hell or high water.

In my own case, I would settle for a Daiwa Millionaire 6HM tournament reel, Penn Magforce rugged surf multiplier and a pair of Spinfisher fixed spools—650SS and 850SS to cover light and heavy work. I cannot think of any beach situation where one of those reels could not cope; and as far as I am concerned, no reel of similar specification from another manufacturer would be a viable alternative.

Stick to the respected names, choose the model most suitable for the way you fish and cast. That is the formula for buying a surf reel. Perhaps the most useful extra recommendation is to buy the best reel you can afford. With a lot of fishing tackle, price does not necessarily reflect quality. With reels it is a general rule that the more you pay the better a reel you get. Performance and handling are involved, but the major advantage of highly priced reels is long service life and satisfactory after sales service. Try finding spares for some Oriental reels only a year old; yet Penn will supply spares for even a 20 year-old Squidder. (And there are plenty of ancient Squidders that have never needed a spare part anyway).

Choosing a fine reel is one step towards good casting and fishing. Straight from the box, even the best reels are improved by careful running-in, proper maintenance and tuning. If necessary, you can rework the mechanics of a reel to lift performance and improve the corrosion resistance of its components. Anglers with workshop facilities are free to make quite substantial modifications.

A word of caution though. There is nothing complicated about the innards of a fishing reel, but its parts are often assembled in strict order. Break that routine, and you smash the reel. Read the instructions, study exploded diagrams, and if in doubt stay within the safety net of limited strip-down. Much of the work detailed here requires little more than taking off sideplates and removing the spool and its bearings.

The finest reel of the wrong kind is a total waste of money. Question One: fixed spool or multiplier?

Throw the reel out of gear and flick the spool. It should be smooth and quiet.

Running-in procedure

New reels should always be carefully run-in. Thrashed at full power from new, any good multiplier will respond fairly well and should not die before middle age. However, reels that continue to run sweetly and reliably from youth to senility were almost certainly eased into operation rather than beaten up from day one. Running-in is a simple process of gradually increasing load on the major components: spool bearings and spindle, gears and bushes.

Running-in techniques are aimed squarely at work-hardening the metal surfaces of a reel. Lathe tools and grinders may produce a superb-looking finish on the moving components, but the metal is still relatively rough. Mating surfaces are accurate and smooth enough to feel right as you spin the reel's handle, but microscopically they are far from perfect. Some abrasion occurs when a new spindle turns on its bearings and gears enmesh under pressure.

Perfection is achieved by operating a reel under modest speed and pressure until the mating parts polish each other and work harden. The reel develops that elusive silky feel, casts and fishes much better, and will carry on working for many years. By contrast, a reel thrashed to the limit without running-in will literally tear itself apart. Though mechanical failure takes months to make itself apparent, the reel never does feel quite right.

Rachets are notoriously weak. Bad rachets jump out of the actuating spring when a fish runs.

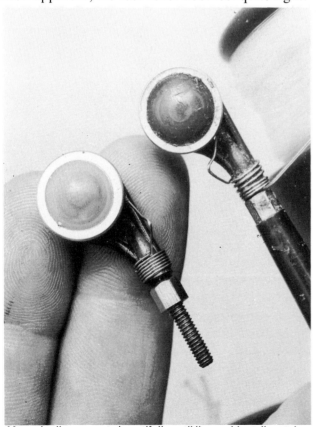

Manual rollers operate beautifully until line accidentally catches the pick-up in mid cast. Always carry a spare.

For obvious reasons, multiplier reels are far more susceptible to mishandling. It is uncommon to see a wide performance variation in fixed spool reels of the same model provided that line height, spool pattern and line diameter are similar. Nothing rotates during the cast; lip friction is highly unlikely to vary between two spools of the same kind. Running-in affects the winding gears only: given careful bedding-in and gradually increased loading, they will outlive the rest of the reel and, just as important, will toughen sufficiently to cope with any sudden excess pressures. Where thrashed gears seize up or strip under the onslaught of a record fish, well run-in components offer that essential margin of insurance. You might never need it, but it is nice to know it exists.

Multiplier tuning is closely linked with running-in. Results vary with makes of reel and spool sizes. Tournament-grade Daiwas and Ambassadeur CTs are particularly vulnerable to premature overload. The difference between a thrashed reel and one progressively work-hardened could be 20 yards. The service life of a spool, gears and bearings might fall between 6 months and 5 years depending on how well you treated the reel in its first month. Differences in casting range are less apparent in the bigger reels, but a well run-in model will last much longer and is less susceptible to sudden shocks.

At some stage your fixed spool reel will need servicing. Some drags are sealed units impossible to repair. Check before you buy—spare spools are very expensive.

Sloppy rotor bearings are a sign of cheap manufacture. No problems on this Penn 750SS.

Teflon, asbestos and other fibres interleave with steel braking plates. If you take the drag apart, be sure to replace the components in the correct order.

Mass manufacturing techniques ensure a fairly good product at worst; most top-quality reels are as close to perfect as anyone could wish. Inevitably, though, a few rogue models creep off the production line and sneak through the quality control network. It pays to run your own tests before buying a new reel. The dealer might not like the idea of your opening up six boxes to find the best reel of the bunch, but it is your money and enjoyment at risk. I would not dream of buying a new reel on the lucky-dip system of taking the first box from the shelf. If there are a dozen reels on the shelf, check them all to find the best, or until you discover the first one which passes all the tests. Multipliers are more critical than fixed spools, but it still pays to wind a few handles before handing over the cash.

Pre-purchase tests

Imperfect spools, twisted frames and poor spindle alignment are major faults in surfcasting multipliers. Spools and bearings can be replaced—but why should you on a new reel? But there is little or no remedy for misalignment; a twisted reel is junk. New ballraces cannot cure a reel whose bearing cups are in the wrong place. Usually such problems are quite obvious from the appearance of the reel and from the way it runs. Bad gears and bent handles are equally simple to spot.

Above all watch out for a reel which is offered as new but really is not. Mail order customers sometimes return goods after using them for a day or two. Thrashed reels go back into stock. Tackle dealers themselves are not averse to fishing with their display goods.

Test 1

Is the reel new? Look it over for signs of salt and abrasion. Open up the reel. Are gears, spindle and bearings filled with the manufacturer's grease or has that been replaced with oil? Sniff the reel: manufacturers do not use WD40 and similar sprays. Fishermen do, and so do people who want to polish up suspect reels for sale. Check screw heads and nuts and bolts. Are they clean cut or tool-damaged? Are there tell-tale specks of sand inside the reel? Reels become shop-soiled easily enough, but they should not be mangled or show evidence of having been on the beach. If you suspect that a reel has been used but is otherwise perfectly sound, try to negotiate a discount and a guarantee. By the same token, a genuine secondhand reel advertised as such is well worth considering if the price is right.

Test 2

Throw the reel out of gear and spin the spool with your finger. Does the main body of the spool run evenly, or do the core and its flanges wobble?

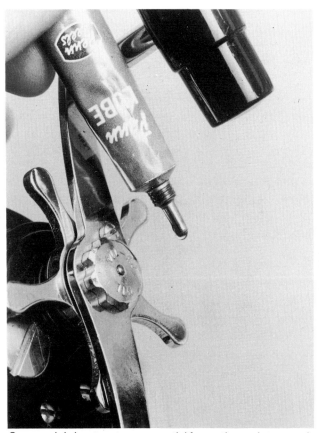

One-way lubricant ports are essential for routine maintenance in the field when you don't want to strip down the mechanism.

Bale arm return springs have a short, tough life. Does your reel's maker supply spares?

54

Reject an obviously 'lumpy' spool. If the spool itself is satisfactory, check how it fits in the reel frame. Spool flanges and reel sideplates should be concentric or very close to it. A revolving spool should not touch any part of the frame.

All good reel makers insist on a perfect fit which eliminates line trapping between spool and frame. Cheaper companies compensate for lower standards by increasing the gap so that spool and frame remain separated even if the spool flange wanders out of alignment. Though the reel may cast fairly well, it tends to trap line in the flange gap. Anglers often wonder how line manages to find its way into such a narrow slot. When the reel spins, the edges of the spool literally suck loose line into the sideplates by a whirlpool of air.

Test 3

A perfect spool set accurately in its frame is virtually a guarantee of bearing and spindle alignment. Loosen the adjustable bearing cap until the spindle develops a slight end-float. Spin the reel and feel how smoothly it runs. Speed is less important than silkiness. Be acutely critical of mechanical harshness transmitted through the reel body. Listen for grating and rubbing sounds. Reject any reel that fails this test.

Strong gears and simple design are most valuable in the long run. Some complex reels fall apart in a few months.

Nearly all reels have an Achilles heel. The Sagarra range is superb in every respect but one: the line-lay gears are weak. However, spares are cheap, so you can afford to carry replacements.

Spools should run quite quickly. However, a new reel is usually filled with cloying grease which masks the free-running qualities of bearings and spindle. Very light spools lack the momentum to spin fast unless filled with line; and no reel ever runs at full speed until correctly run in. So long as there is no obvious mechanical fault in the reel, speed should not concern you. In fact the reverse is usually the case: most reels are inherently too free-running and must be governed down for casting even on the tournament court. If you like, clean off excess bearing grease and re-check the running speed.

The exception is where a reel sounds quiet and feels smooth but is so slow that the spool hardly rotates in response to a heavy flick. The bearings and frame may well be out of alignment. Loosen the sideplate security screws about half a turn. Does the reel now spin faster? If so, alignment is definitely suspect. Remember to back off the bearing cap tension before you run the test, otherwise results are meaningless. It also helps to clean out packing grease, another cause of false readings in small reels. In extreme cases, frame and sideplates will look warped; but it takes only a fraction of an inch distortion to destroy a multiplier's performance. There are plenty more reels available, so why take the risk?

Test 4

Check the operation of gears, drag, handle, rachet and any other features which may affect life and performance: reel stand security, chrome-plating, no cracks in plastic components, no dents and corrosion in metal plates and covers. Basically, if it looks right and operates smoothly, the reel is almost certainly acceptable. Fixed spool tests really extend no further than this. Beware of flimsy bale arm wires and frozen line rollers. Check the quality of rotating aluminium castings that support the bale assembly. A sloppy fit and side-play indicate poor design. There is every chance that the drive spindle also runs unevenly and loosely in its bearings. If so, main gears will overload and wear out. In extreme cases teeth jump out of mesh under load.

Test 5

This is not a test of quality or mechanical soundness. In its way, though, it is more important than the other tests combined. Is the reel suitable for your style of fishing? Tuning and running-in cannot transform one type of reel into another. Tournament casting and lightweight fishing multipliers never offer the same rugged fighting power as a purpose-built heavy surfcasting reel. A 300 yard/25 pound test model built for dragging 50 pound channel bass and conger by the snout will not cast 250 yards unless you happen to be Superman. On a more mundane note, it is no good buying a multiplier reel of any kind unless you are prepared to devote time and practice to mastering it. You need a big fixed spool reel instead.

Thousands of newcomers and ill-advised fishermen walk out of the shop with a beautiful reel which is totally inappropriate for their way of fishing. Some dealers help, but too many of them do not really give a damn what you buy. The rule is never to part with a penny unless you are absolutely certain the reel is exactly what you need to fish the surf. If you don't know, ask around and try to borrow a selection of reels to test. At the end of the day, it is your decision and your money. Mistakes can easily cost £50–£75.

Reels: Running In and Maintenance

Expert fishermen argue about the best way to run in a new reel. Some consider that you should strip down and relubricate a new reel before loading it with line. Others, myself included, prefer to start the bedding-in process beforehand. In the old days, it certainly was better to check the mechanism, regrease gears and lubricate spindles. Most reels were full of metal swarf; the lubricants were chosen simply to protect the reel during transit and storage. Often it amounted to no more than a skim of thick grease over the gear wheels. Bearings and spool spindles were almost dry.

Modern reels are adequately pre-lubricated and free from heavy swarf. Sometimes gears and drive components are lubricated for life and thus better left alone. The gear case on a fixed spool reel is stuffed with grease and, barring accidents, should not require attention for at least a year. Why make extra work for yourself?

Look inside the reel: make sure there are no chunks of scrap metal floating in the grease. As a precaution, add a drop of thick oil to the spindle ends and bearing cups. Check that the blocks are in position (centrifugal braking systems only) and adjust the spool tension to give perceptible end-float on the spindle. Load the reel and go fishing.

It is unrealistic to expect a brand new, tight reel to run at full speed. Be prepared for moderate casting performance, and do not try to force the pace. Deliberately reduce casting power, set the drag to modest pressure, and wind in steadily. After fishing, wash the outside of the reel free of salt and grit. Open it up and add a dab of grease or oil where necessary. Next time you fish, gently increase the casting pressure. Work on the theory that it takes at least 100 casts to polish bearing and spindle surfaces. During this period, which may take a couple of days or 3 months, depending on how often you cast, keep the reel clean but do not worry about tuning it for speed. Live with modest casting performance a little longer. In the long run patience pays big dividends.

After 100 casts in the 100–125 yard bracket, most reels are bedded down well enough to accept a reasonable increase in casting force. Before that can be achieved, you must tune the mechanism to flow more easily. At the same time, re-lubricate the main gears as well; 100 casts later, most reels should be work-hardened and ready for maximum power.

Strip-down and lubrication

Strictly speaking it is rarely necessary to strip a reel beyond its main components: frame, sideplates and spool. However, I prefer to make a thorough job at this stage, then I do not have to worry about another complete stripdown for at least 3 months. Work carefully and refer to the maker's diagrams. Lay the parts in sequence on a sheet of clean

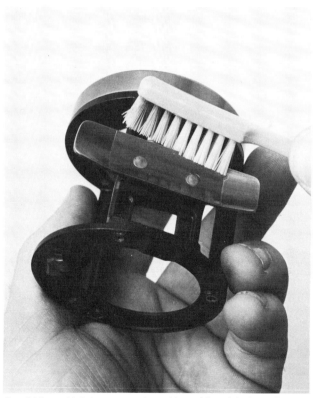

Scrubbing with hot water and an old toothbrush is the only way to get rid of encrusted salt and grit.

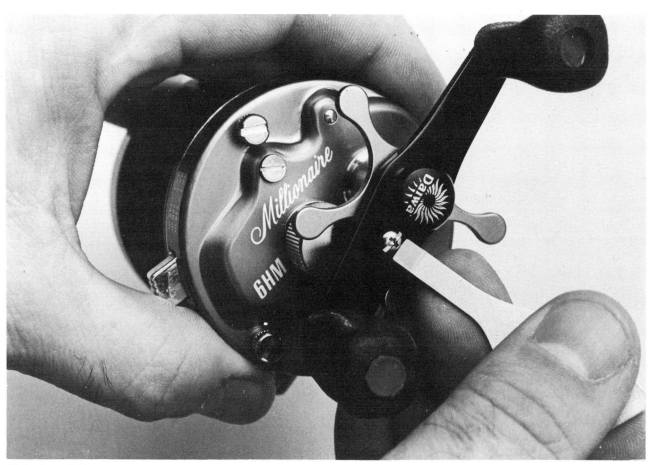

Strip down 1. Take off the screw that holds the handle nut locking plate.

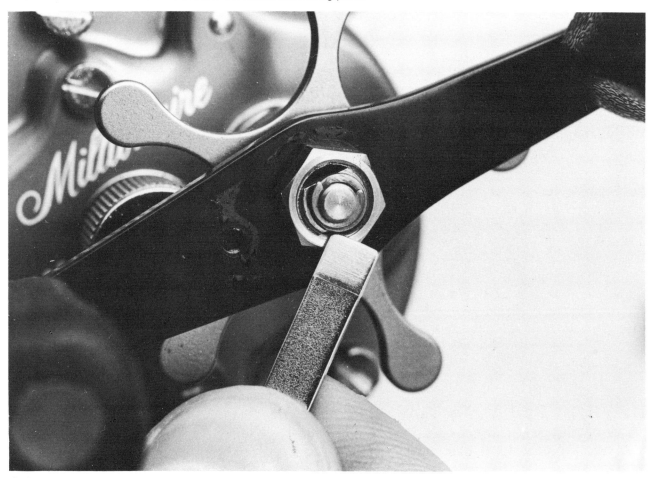

Strip down 2. Push off the circlip on the end of the main drive shaft.

absorbent paper. Most work can be done with the multi-purpose wrench/screwdriver supplied with the reel. Daiwa and Penn tools are versatile enough to strip a reel to the bone. Lubricants are wide open to personal preference. I like Teflon or Molydenum grease for gears, waterproof grease for the handle and SAE 20/50 or thin machine oil for spindle and bearings. One spot of lubricant in the right place is more effective than a handful splashed in the general area. A well set-up reel looks almost dry inside.

Strip-down and lubrication are essentially the same in routine maintenance as they are for running-in and tuning. Thorough cleansing is essential before routine oiling and greasing; day-to-day maintenance demands no more than taking out the spool to expose major internal units and bearings. Adjust the following schedule accordingly. It is the grand banquet—and usually a snack will do. Much of the work is based on the Daiwa Millionaire and the Penn 970, which are representative of the majority of good reels on the market.

STAGE 1: Clean the exterior of the reel.
Gently wipe away sand and salt. Flow hot water over sideplates and frame, and scour off stubborn particles with an old toothbrush. Squirting a powerful spray of water on to a reel merely forces dirt and salt inside. Tape, tie or rubber band the free end of the line to the spool, shake off excess water, and leave the reel to dry out for an hour in an airing cupboard.

STAGE 2: Take off the sideplate.
Modern Penns, most Ambassadeur and Daiwa reels feature quick take-apart screws on the right-hand sideplate cover. Loosen the screws—which are a captive-fit so you do not lose them—and pull off the sideplate. Gently remove the spool. Be careful not to drop the centrifugal brake blocks. A few reels like the Ambassadeur 9000C take apart from the left-hand side. Newell 220 and 229 reels are better stripped from the left because then the left-hand ballrace is less likely to drop out and fall in the dust. Older Penn reels are either stripped from the right-hand side by taking out the sideplate and frame screws (usually 6) or by loosening a single locking screw before undoing the bayonet fitting.

STAGE 3: Clean and check the spool.
Wipe spool flanges and spindle ends. Examine the spool for cracks and the spindle for rough edges and signs of excessive wear. Check the brake blocks—they often split—and clean their support

bar. As a matter of routine, there is little more to be done. Once a year, strip off all the line and examine the inside faces of the spool for pressure damage and corrosion. Handle spools carefully. Dropping them to the floor may crack flanges or distort spindles.

STAGE 4: Remove the spindle bearings.
Guard your bearings jealously. One speck of sand or a drop of saltwater may destroy them. On modern reels the ballraces are supported by removable caps on the sideplates. Unscrew the caps by hand or carefully with a screwdriver. Most reel manufacturers apart from Penn allow the ballrace to float in its cap; packing shims are used for adjustment and alignment. Be careful not to drop a ballrace or to lose track of shim combinations. Be particularly careful about the pressure plate that controls spool tension. Penn use a sealed cap/bearing unit with an internal spring plate. It is more difficult to clean and lubricate but is neater and a great deal tougher.

After the initial run-in period and periodically thereafter—every 3 months—it is wise to flush out and relubricate. Lubricants do break down after a time, either by burning up or absorbing saltwater, and cannot be expected to safeguard bearings forever. Day-to-day topping up is always necessary to maintain lubricant levels and to smooth the cast. On older reels without blocks and magnets, lubricant viscosity is all that stands between you and a monumental backlash.

Solvents are generally unnecessary, but in extreme cases you could use petrol or Gunk. Soak bearings in a jar of solvent, or squirt them with a medical syringe. Normally, flush out the old oil with a stream of fresh lubricant.

If a ballrace is detachable from its cap, try this simple alternative. Drop the bearings into a dessert spoon, cover them with fresh oil, and *gently* heat the spoon over a gas or radiant ring. Old oil melts out; fresh oil percolates inside. The same technique re-impregnates solvent treated bearings—but do not try it before the petrol has fully evaporated.

Saturate the ballraces, then drain off excess lubricant. Reassemble the caps and shims, then store the assembly well out of the way. There is no point putting caps back inside a reel which is still full of muck and old grease.

Solvents are essential for checking the state of old bearings. Wash out every scrap of lubricant so that the ballrace runs in metal-to-metal contact. It should still spin smoothly and quietly. Bearings that grate or clatter should be replaced.

Given adequate bedding-in time and reasonable

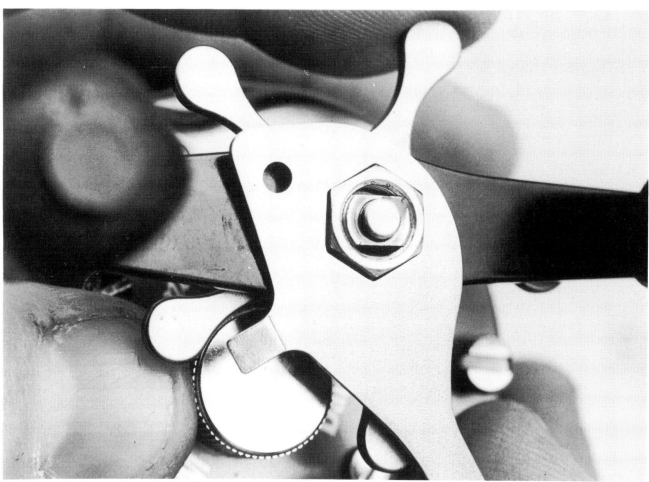

Strip down 3. *Unscrew the main handle nut.*

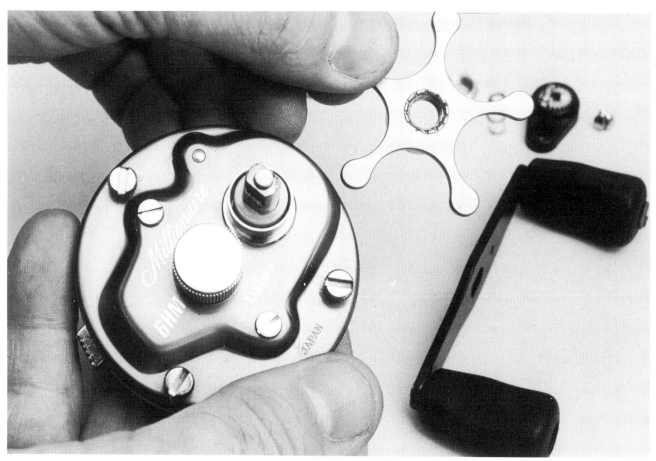

Strip down 4. *Unwind the star drag and take out the two screws holding the sideplate cover to the inner plate.*

Strip down 5. *Lift off the plate. Clean the mechanism as necessary. Look for broken gear teeth and other signs of excessive wear.*

Strip down 6. *The spindle pinion is responsible for poor casting. Check the sleeve for tightness. Clean out old grease.*

care, a set of ballraces should last as long as the rest of the reel. Most failures are due either to abuse or to the wrong lubricants. Some anglers intent on the last ounce of speed squirt in WD40 and watery Teflon or silicon-based additives. They are not intended for this kind of work; the bearings rip themselves apart. Spares are available at high cost from the reel manufacturer. A specialist bearing supplier may, however, stock a suitable replacement, which could be of a higher quality—and half the price.

STAGE 5: Strip down the left hand plate.

The left-hand plate is usually secured by 4–6 slotted screws. Take them right out and make a note of their lengths and positions. Screws threaded into the main frame crossbars are usually longer than the pair attached to the reel stand. They are not interchangeable.

Pull off the side plate. Wash out plain plastic covers in hot soapy water. Bearing cup sleeves and rachet assembly on simple reels like the Penn Squidder are made from brass or stainless steel. Water does them no harm. Afterwards apply a smear of grease or thick oil to the sliding surfaces.

Pressed or machined metal sideplates can be flushed with soapy water, Gunk petrol or paraffin.

Dry them, then wipe the entire surfaces with waterproof grease, silicon jelly or wax-based coating like Waxoyl, a motor vehicle spray-on underseal. Only a *smear* is used. Keep it away from level wind drive wheels, bearings and rachets. It is a fiddly job to coat every corner of the sideplate's interior but there is no other method of slowing down corrosion. Alloy sideplates are wide open to saltwater attack. Usually they rot from the inside outwards.

Finally, examine the level-wind drive gear and lubricate its support axle with a spot of thin oil. On big ABUs, clean out the brake block mechanism and check the blocks. The Penn magnetic controller threaded into the left-hand plate needs no maintenance, though it does no harm to run a film of oil over the magnet's face.

STAGE 6: Frame maintenance.

Most frames are of unit construction. Penns are screwed together; ABUs are pressed and brazed Daiwas are die-cast in aluminium. They are all quite good—provided the frame and sideplates are squarely aligned with the spool. Corrosion is a major problem, so frames must be washed after every trip. Afterwards, squirt on WD40 to drive out moisture; inject a little waterproof grease into

Strip down 7. *The anti-reverse mechanism tends to slip out of alignment when the reel comes apart. Make sure it is clipped back before you assemble the reel.*

Strip down 8. *Coat the sideplate with waterproof grease to counteract saltwater corrosion.*

Strip down 9. *The left hand sideplate. Check the rachet system and lubricate the level wind drive cog. The plate itself must be coated to prevent corrosion.*

the screw holes. Preventative maintenance is your only hope.

STAGE 7: Stripping down the drive unit.

This is the frightening part. Fishermen live in mortal dread of stripping down the right-hand side of their multipliers. Penns are deceptive. They look so easy to strip, and they do slide apart easily. Now try getting the thing back together. If you know the trick of rotating the brass 'D' shaped internal plate, go ahead. Otherwise, leave it to the experts. A Penn is so tough inside and so easily lubricated that full strip-down is unnecessary unless a component is broken. Why tempt fate?

Most other reels are easier to work on. The same broad technique handles them all. First, make sure the gear lever is in its engaged position. Lay the sideplate inside face down on a clean towel. Towelling is a soft but steady base to work from, and any bits that fly out of the reel are trapped. There is nothing worse than grubbing around on the kitchen floor for a missing spring. Nine times out of ten you never find it.

1) Remove the grub screw that secures the handle drive nut. Sometimes the screw butts directly against the nut faces, more often it operates on an anchor plate surrounding the nut. Take off the handle nut as well.

2) The tip of the exposed drive shaft sports a screw or nut and a circlip. Detach both—and make sure the circlip does not fly into orbit. Now lift off the handle.

3) Unscrew the star drag wheel and lift it off. Note the position and exact order of spring washers which may be above and/or below the star wheel. If a plain collar follows the star wheel, take that off as well. Sometimes it stays deep down on the shaft, in which case leave it alone.

4) Remove the screws that attach the cover-plate. Lift off the cover to expose the internal workings of the reel. Most drive mechanisms are of unit construction, so nothing will spring off. However, it pays to keep the reel face down on the

Strip down 10. Wipe the inner faces of the reel to remove sand and salt. A stray grain of sand will mark the spool and ruin performance.

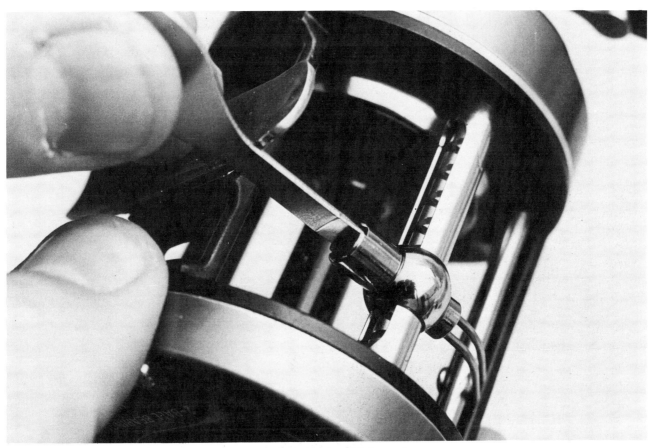

Strip down 11. *Open the level wind guide cover and check the thread follower for wear.*

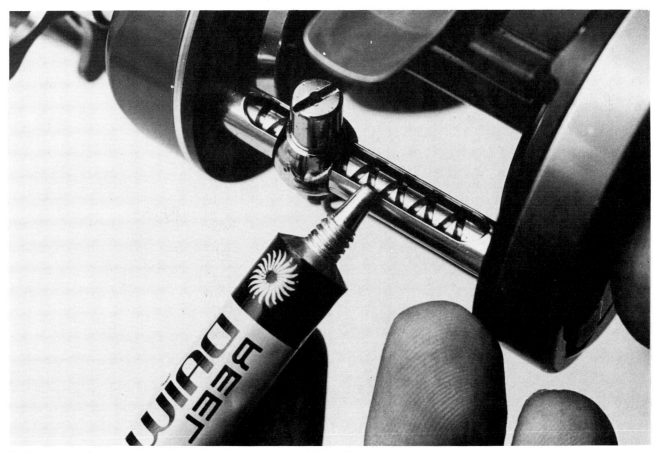

Strip down 12. *Lubricate the endless thread with a smear of light oil.*

Strip down 13. *Oil the ballraces with thin lubricant.*

towel. The worst problem is that drag washers and main drive gear lift up when you take off the coverplate. If they come away altogether, refer to the instruction book for replacement details. Otherwise, press the whole unit back down its shaft. Unless drag washers are burned out or a gear is broken, leave well alone. Watch out for the anti-reverse dog and washer at the base of the shaft. If it drops out of engagement the reel will either seize up or rotate in both directions.

5) Gently clean out the old lubricant—using solvents if necessary—and relubricate sparingly with grease. Keep grease away from the inside of the sliding pinion that drives the spool spindle. Make absolutely certain that no mineral grease or solvent strays into the drag assembly.

6) Clean out the inside face of the cover and coat it in grease or Waxoyl. Though less exposed than the other sideplate, the drive side cover is prey to saltwater corrosion and must be protected.

Its anodised layer is not sufficiently tough.

7) Rebuild the right-hand side of the reel by reversing the strip-down procedure. No force is required. If the components fail to seat perfectly, it is because you have gone wrong. Watch out for the anti-reverse dog, the gear lever and that drive shaft circlip. It goes back *after* the handle is in place. A bit left over? Probably the spring washer from between the star drag and handle.

8) In the event of some mechanical failure inside the reel, take out the broken component and order a new one either by sending back the old piece or, better still, by looking up the part number in the catalogue. Do not try to describe the part. Handles, spools and bearings are easy enough; washers, drag plates and gears are another matter. It is even more confusing when a reel is available in standard and high-speed versions or if two reels are quite similar—like the ABU 9000C and its cousin the ABU 12.

Reels: Tuning and Modification Aids

Basic maintenance and lubrication, correct line load and built-in cast controllers ensure adequate reel performance. Even in standard form a modern surfcasting multiplier or fixed spool reel more than equals the average man's casting and fishing skills. Tuning and modification are unnecessary in the strictly practical sense.

Surfcasting is a fascinating subject which extends far beyond bread and butter techniques of casting baits and winding in fish. Tackle itself provides endless scope for self expression and technical advancement. Even if you cannot cast hard enough to push a reel to its limits, it is still interesting to experiment; because no reel is ever perfect, there is ample opportunity to improve its strength, service life and performance. Some modifications demand special equipment and workshop skills. Most rely on bolt-on accessories and simple alterations well within the realms of the household tool kit. A piece of oil-soaked abrasive paper wrapped around a matchstick might be the key to an extra 10 yards on your cast.

Replacement spools

The present generation of multiplier spools are either pressed from sections of aluminium alloy or machine cut from a solid block. A single-piece spool is inevitably stronger and more precise, but even the pressed version is sweeter running and more reliable than older types of plastic spool. Plastic spools explode under severe nylon line pressure; very few run without some wobble and vibration. Back in the early days of British tournament casting we sorted through perhaps fifty plastic spools to find just two that ran perfectly.

Aware of the inherent problems of Penn plastic spools, Carl Newell of California manufactures a range of replacement spools in die-cast alloy. Strong, precise and far more reliable than Penn's original spool, they enhance the performance of Surfmaster and Squidder surf reels. The only drawback is that Newell spools are made in sections. Under extreme pressure they too can open up.

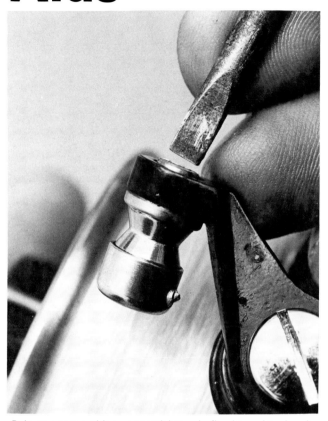

Bale arm removal is an essential step in fixed spool tuning. It throws a great strain on the line roller. Check security and if necessary lock the support threads with Loctite.

High-quality drags are designed not to lock up. Some threads are soon stripped by excess pressure. Use an external spool locking system instead.

Penn themselves awoke to the Achilles heel in their popular casting reels. Squidders and Surfmasters of all sizes are now available with a single piece aluminium alloy spool as standard. Modified reels carry an 'L' suffix—146L and 140L in the case of Squidders. Spare spools are freely available, and may be fitted into older Penns. Though a little heavier than the plastic casting spool, new alloy spools are fairly tame if you squirt thick lubricant into the bearings. Try STP oil additive. As well as running smoothly and accurately, these new 'L' spools are almost indestructible. Corrosion apart, there is little to go wrong. Line capacity is a slight improvement on the plastic spool, and there is no need for soft backing.

Owners of ABU Ambassadeur 6000C and 6500C series reels are acutely aware of the limited resilience of the standard spool which easily distorts under load and may explode. Spools from the DAM Champion 800B reel are very close to a perfect fit in some Ambassadeurs. Because of variations in manufacturing tolerances, you cannot guarantee an acceptable match, but it is worth testing the idea. The DAM spool is extremely well made, tough and sweet-running—vastly superior to the standard ABU product.

A few anglers make their own spools from solid

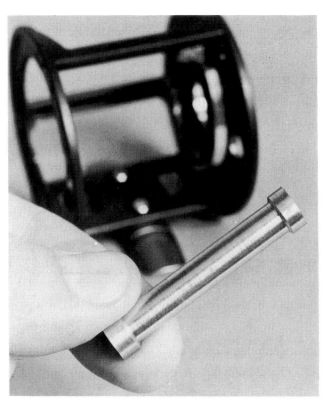

Unless the reel is used for very light fishing, level wind removal must be followed by cage replacement. A simple brass crossbar screwed across the level wind position holds the reel rigid and true.

aluminium alloy. For the man with lathe experience it is easy work. The spindle is more of a problem than the main body of the spool, and it usually pays to build a new spool around a spindle cut from an old production model.

At the other extreme, a few anglers regard ABU 8000C and 9000C spools as slightly too heavy and slow for the reel. They drill a pattern of holes in the flanges, thus reducing weight without seriously weakening the spool. It is slow, painstaking work unless you have access to a lathe or drill press fitted with a dividing attachment which accurately reproduces the hole patterns. One hole in the wrong spot will destroy spool balance.

Replacement handles

Manufacturers of smaller tournament-grade reels originally aimed their products at the freshwater baitcasting market. Small handles are perfectly suited to that kind of work, where pressures are low and distances seldom exceed 50 yards. Cranking 250 yards of line across the seabed with a tiny handle is sheer murder. Special power handles are available for most popular reels. They work quite well but introduce a problem of their own. The extra leverage encourages direct cranking in circumstances where pumping is much easier on the reel. In extreme cases handle pressure and excessive line tension overload the reel. The gears are the weak spot, and their teeth

Newell seat and crossbars improve the performance of old-style Penn reels. New Penns now incorporate stronger frames and one-piece alloy spools.

Bale arm triggering pressure is adjustable on reels like this DAM5000. The high setting may be sufficient to prevent mid-cast bale closure; if so, you don't have to cut off the wire.

A stepped washer helps improve line coning on fixed spool reels. Either use washers or, in the case of the DAM saltwater reels, dial in the appropriate setting.

shear off or jump out of mesh. On the whole, though, a power handle makes more sense than the tiny wrist-snapper fitted as standard.

New reel frames

Newell produce a series of frame modifications which overcome the inherent weakness of old Penn crossbars. Newell bars and reel stands are a most valuable accessory for older reels. Unfortunately they corrode like mad. Modification of modern Penns is unnecessary because the company has switched to a different frame design which is at least as good as Newell and, in the usual Penn tradition, virtually immune to saltwater attack.

Replacement and modified cages are an essential aspect of tournament casting. Small ABU and Daiwa reels dominate the casting scene, but must first be modified to remove the level wind mechanism. Level winds reduce line capacity and cut distance. They also prevent maximum power input: the top crossbar gets in the way of your thumb, so that a firm grip on the spool is impossible.

ABU make a special plain frame for the 6000 and 6500 series reels. Called the CT cage, it is available through tackle shops or direct from the company's spares outlet. Fitting is a 5 minute job involving just a screwdriver. Existing spools fit the CT cage.

However, there is no reason why a level-wind cage cannot be modified. Take off the level wind bar and guide, plus the drive gear in the left-hand side plate. Cut off the top crossbar for thumb clearance, and insert a solid stiffening rod where the level wind guide came out. A suitable bar can be machined from stainless steel or brass, and is screwed securely across the frame. The same technique applies to Daiwa and other level-wind reels for which a CT cage is not commercially available. Some tackle shops sell converted reels or offer to modify the angler's own reel. Kits and conversions tend to be expensive for what little is involved, but they do save time, particularly if the alternative is to look for a friendly lathe operator who can machine the necessary stiffening piece.

Gears and drive pinions

Newell replacement gears are available for many Penn reels. They may have some worthwhile application in the offshore game fishing reels, but certainly appear to offer little advantage for surfcasting. It is not so much that Penn are particularly weak and Newell significantly stronger. The Newell gear probably is a little tougher, but in the long run it is the design limitation of small multipliers that sets the pace.

Gear wheel diameter and tooth size limit the potential strength of any surf reel. The higher the gear ratio, the less the margin of safety. In other words, no matter how hard one tries, small multiplier gears turn out to be quite weak; to some extent material and tempering count for little. The only answer is to run in the reel and use it with reasonable care—in practical terms, pump the rod rather than crank the handle.

Drive pinions are also notoriously fragile, but their main fault is excessive drag on the spool spindle. The pinion retracts into the sideplate to free the spool for casting. Fine . . . but it does not prevent the pinion from rotating with the spindle or from acting as a brake drum. A pinion must not be so tight that it fouls the spindle: merely touching it rips yards from the cast. Check pinion and spindle for friction. Excessive drag is easily felt. In some cases you must strip down the reel, take out the pinion, reassemble the frame and sideplates, then spin the reel. If the pinion is even fractionally tight, the spool will now freewheel for much longer. The solution is simple. Polish out the pinion hole. Proper reamers and laps ensure a perfect cure, but you can come very close with abrasive paper wrapped around a matchstick.

Polishing the innards may make the reel run better. Friction between spool spindle and drive pinion is a common cause of poor results.

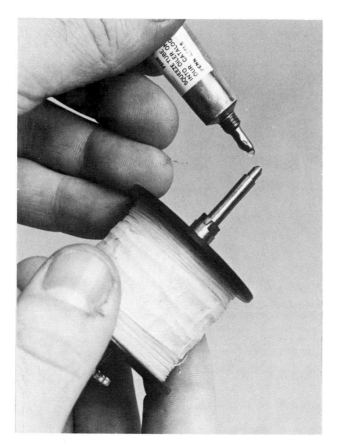

Experiment with a range of oils to find those that best suit your reel and the way you cast.

The spiral spring behind the Penn 970's control magnet can be removed to give extra control. Good casters benefit from the new low setting which may add 20 yards to the cast.

70

Use the finest grade of wet-and-dry paper soaked in thin oil. Work carefully and with featherweight pressure. Polish up the hole so that it enlarges by a few thousandths of an inch only. Clean it out, check the fit, then burnish with a strand of cloth soaked in metal polish. At a guess I would say that at least half our surfcasting reels are affected by pinion friction to some degree—say 5–10 yards on a 175 yard cast.

Drags

The drag (clutch, brake or whatever you care to call it) is a menance. Not one mass-produced beach reel, fixed spool or multiplier, excels in this department. Penn's Magpower reel is fitted with a Senator-based drag which has been around long enough to prove reasonably reliable. Daiwa drags are quite good to start with, but tend to fade to insignificance after a time. Some accessory manufacturers—including Newell—offer replacement packs for popular multipliers and fixed spools. Most are acceptable; but I think their superiority is largely an illusion. They seem better than they really are simply because anything must be an improvement on the chewed up, heat blackened discs you took out. You might just as well use the reel manufacturer's own spares.

Fixed spool drags are more critical. On multipliers it is usually possible to compensate for poor drag washers by backing off on the tension, so that the drag operates smoothly, then add extra pressure by thumbing the spool. Much depends on the size and speed of fish; but on the whole it is a practical proposition. Not so with a fixed spool. Thumbing is imprecise and difficult. Backwinding—paying out line by turning the reel backwards—is strictly for lightweight tackle and puny species. The average tope or channel bass would rip your knuckles off.

Unfortunately, really good braking systems make a fixed spool reel almost impossible to cast hard. The drag washers prevent the spool from locking up. However, it is unsafe to cast without locking the reel. If the spool rotates under full casting power, line cuts your finger. Fishermen tend to screw down the drag until it does lock, then they leave it there. When they hook a big fish and slacken the drag, the washers are fused together, which means the brake is either fully on or off.

Never abuse a fine drag system. It is far better to modify the reel so that the spool may be locked without resorting to the drag nut. Drill a hole in the spool and use a wire locking clip anchored to the reel frame, as detailed in the photographs. Aesthetically it is a mess; in practice it locks the reel firmly and extends drag life and reliability.

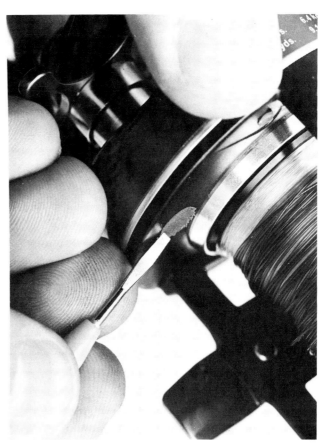

Taking out level wind mechanisms sometimes leaves gaping holes in the reel frame. Rubber inserts prevent saltwater invasion and protect the delicate internal mechanisms.

Species of fish like the false albacore are more easily hooked on light tackle and small lures; 6–10 pound line would be about right for working lures along the surfline. Albacores hit hard and run like torpedoes, and their initial attack highlights a serious fault in fixed spool reel design. The drag cannot accelerate quickly enough to prevent a sudden build up of pressure that may snap the line.

Setting the drag to minimum pressure helps enormously, and there is some advantage in 'slippery' washers which literally skid one on another. Some surf fishermen squirt WD40-type lubricant into the drag washers so that they do slide rapidly into action when the fish first hits. Unwanted lubricant is soon thrown out or burned up.

Cast controls

A good many fishermen modify and tune their multiplier reels to prevent or minimise backlash. As long as brakes are not used to compensate for atrocious casting technique, there is no harm in running a few experiments. Looking at it from the other direction, really good casters can tune a reel to gain speed even at the expense of control. All things are possible as long as you recognise the limitations of the reel's basic design. All multipliers are potentially uncontrollable, and the more you extend their performance the less room there is for error. Backlash may not be a significant factor. If a tournament champion can wring an extra 10 yards from the cast at the expense of, say, a one in three chance of backlash, he is happy enough. On the other hand, an inexperienced angler might jump at the chance of 5 good casts out of 6 even if the tuning process does swallow 15 percent of his casting power.

Small, light spools are easier to cast than a heavy one crammed with 250 yards or more of thick nylon. It helps to use the smallest reel you can get away with. Excessive weight and diameter decrease the initial acceleration of the spool from rest, then exaggerate the flywheel effect which causes line over-spill.

All spools are capable of running fast enough to backlash. Some are inherently more docile than others, so design and construction do play a part in safe casting. Line level and diameter are also involved: within reason, the less line and the thicker it is, the faster the spool empties and the less chance there is of a backlash. Good casting style and rod design do much to eliminate ragged power flow—and roughness alone is responsible for the majority of backlashes. In all, design and

tackle matching contribute the lion's share to multiplier control. Tuning whether by oil viscosity or with inbuilt controllers is really a fine adjustment. Approach it from that angle for the best results.

OILS ultimately determine the maximum speed of a reel in response to any given casting power. The thicker the oil, the slower the spool responds. Oil's effect increases in step with spool speed and casting power. The braking effect of SAE 90 or 140 grade gear oil—very thick and restrictive—is greater during a 150 yard cast than at 50 yards. Water-thin machine oil has virtually no braking effect at any speed. The vast majority of surf reels are uncontrollable if thus lubricated.

The best technique is to start with thick oil—SAE 90 is excellent—then step down in small stages until you discover the oil which exactly matches your style and casting power. Bait drag, air temperature and wind affect the results; thick oil is useful in summer, lighter grades compensate for icy weather. A useful progression of oils is 10/50 engine oil, SAE30, SAE90 and finally syrupy STP when all else fails. Ultra-fussy casters fill in the gaps with home-made dilutions. SAE90 added to an equal part of SAE30 provides an

Spool end float is extremely important. No reel casts well that is restricted by a tight bearing cap.

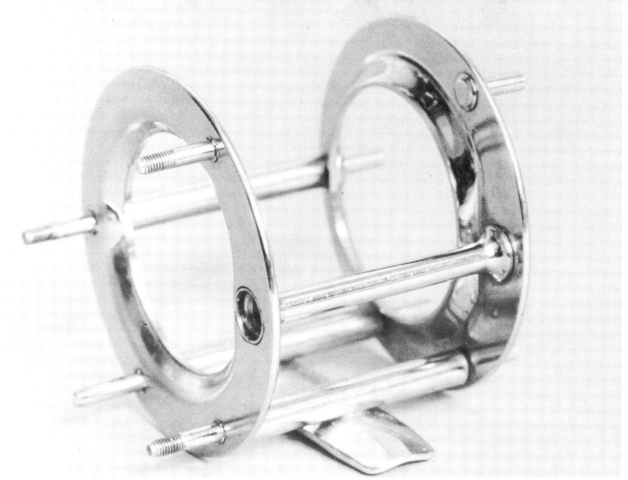

The ABU Ambassadeur CT cage fits most 6000 and 6500 series reels. A plain crossbar replaces the level wind. "CT" reels are favourites in the tournament world.

intermediate stage between the two straight oils.

Oil viscosity is used mainly to control reels without special braking systems. If a reel has a centrifugal brake or magnet, use thin oil in the bearings, then dial in the right amount of control with block size or magnet position. A change of oils may provide a mid-way point between one size of block and the next, but on the whole it is used as a lubricant pure and simple.

BRAKE BLOCKS are best chosen on the trial and error principle. There are few worthwhile tuning modifications available. You could try using plastic blocks instead of fibre. Plastic blocks are more slippery and might produce a braking force unobtainable with fibre. Sharpening the blocks to reduce contact has no effect, since it is the weight of the block and its coefficient of friction that determine the outcome, not its area in contact with the brake drum.

Cutting blocks in half is perfectly acceptable. You will reduce the braking force that way, though with a slight risk of splitting the material. It is better to grind fibre blocks, although plastic can be successfully hacksawed. It is unnecessary to use the same number and sizes of block on each arm of the brake spindle; spools do not fly out of balance.

Modern Ambassadeur baitcasting reels use an 'improved' brake block system which most competent anglers find detrimental. Plastic blocks

are clipped on to a special bar positioned across the spool end, but unlike the old bars which were parallel, these are built up at the ends to prevent blocks sliding too far and falling off. The drawback is that you cannot use tiny blocks—and one small block is the ideal tuning weight for tournament-grade casting. The only solution—tedious but often essential—is to drill out the bar and insert a parallel one which marries up to the older fibre blocks. Old style spools will not interchange with modern ABU designs unless the spindle ends are reworked.

MAGNETIC CONTROLS are set with a few turns of the screwdriver. For routine fishing no modifications are necessary. Simply dial in the braking power necessary to control the cast and overcome headwinds.

Penn's magnetic brake is specially chosen to accommodate the widest cross section of surf anglers who fish in all kinds of conditions with tackle ranging from light lures to 12 ounce sinkers and a half mullet bait. Penn trades off reel speed in return for safe casting for the majority. Even at its lowest setting the magnet has quite an effect on the spool, more so on the smaller 970 reel. However, a small modification or two adds a new surge of power to the cast.

Take off the left-hand sideplate and screw the magnet inwards until it falls out of its threads. Catch the retaining spring which pops out.

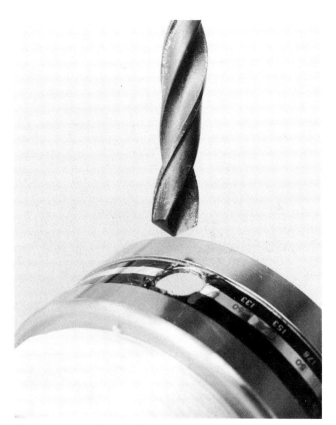

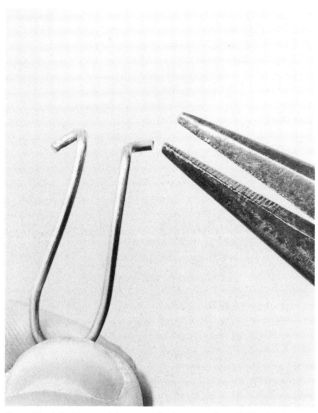

Spool lock 1. Drill a small hole in the spool rim.

Spool lock 2. Use stainless steel wire to make a "U" with hooks.

Spool lock 3. Secure to the reel stalk with heavy nylon.

Spool lock 4. Before casting, lock the spool to the reel frame with the hook. Now there is no need to tighten the drag screw.

Replace the magnet but not the spring, then rebuild the reel. Wound fully *out*, the magnet now gains the extra 1.75 turns of thread previously occupied by the spring. The braking effect is substantially reduced. Most competent casters can easily accommodate the extra speed and could gain up to 20 yards. For the ultimate state of tune, machine down the inner flange of the housing so that the magnet can be set even further out from the spool. This way it is possible to make the reel run uncontrollably fast. Should the magnet housing prove unstable once the retaining spring is out, press a strip of tape across the screw slot and reel sideplate.

Machining a fixed-spool rim

Front lips of fixed spool reels are responsible for a great deal of line friction during the cast. Some spools can be improved by machining away the excess metal until only a thin lip remains. This is polished to a mirror finish. There is no need to re-profile spool lips for general fishing, but a tournament caster usually gains a few extra yards. Just 5 yards could make the difference between winning and joining the also-rans. The only point

to watch is that in mounting the spool in a lathe you must ensure that the rim turns accurately, otherwise the new front lip loses concentricity with the bale rotor and the back of the spool.

New spools and permanent arbors

LONG DISTANCE CASTING gives full details on spool profiling for maximum casting range with fixed spools. Compensating arbors are usually hand-wound from old nylon line, but once you have determined the shape of the arbor it is better to make one from machined plastic or aluminium alloy cut into mating halves which are glued around the spool core.

A logical extension of the theory is to make a completely new spool, much shallower than standard. The bottom half of a normal spool is occupied by backing—wasted space and a definite contribution to bad line loading. A custom-made spool reduces waste and promotes better performance, particularly if the spool base is cut into an arbor profile.

Roller and bale arm replacement

Bale arm wires and line rollers are a nuisance, the

75

Like most reels, the Sagarra Tarzan suffers from excessive lip friction. Machining the lip then polishing it reduces friction and lengthens the cast.

great weakness of every fixed spool reel. Cutting off a bale wire and re-setting the arm roller angle help reduce snap-offs in mid cast and produce a positive cone of line on the spool. Apart from that, or resetting the spool base washers as an alternative means of coning the line, there is little to be done with a fixed spool unless you are particularly ingenious. One excellent accessory has recently come on to the market. George Shingleton

of Hull, England makes a folding replacement for the Mitchell 498/499's manual roller pick-up. Instead of getting in the way during a cast, the new roller folds back and locks the rotor against the reel stand. Casts are smoother and trouble-free, and the spool remains in a fully extended position, which in theory at least is ideal for maximum performance.

Make Your Own Sinkers

Backlashes, wear and tear on the line, rocks and weeds buried in the seabed ensure that no sinker lasts for ever. Life expectancy is probably no more than two or three fishing trips. Plenty of beaches are a graveyard for terminal tackle, and you might lose a sinker every other cast.

Losing tackle is part of the game. From a cash point of view it makes sense to minimise the risk, and the best solution is to invest in a set of moulds. Home-made 5 ounce sinkers costs a few pence even if you have to buy the lead; commercially produced sinkers are around ten times more expensive and often not as good.

Casual fishermen probably would not recover the outlay on a set of two or three moulds. If you use half a dozen sinkers a year, buy them. Twelve or twenty sinkers cost as much as a pair of moulds and a few yards of wire, so if you use more than that in a season, do-it-yourself definitely repays the investment.

Home moulding encourages better fishing. If sinkers cost 50 pence each, you will not want to cast them into rocks where the recovery rate is less than 50/50. Faced with that prospect, a beach angler would almost certainly move to cleaner ground . . . and often lose contact with his fish. Cod and bass love rocks and weed, and successful fishing means taking a calculated gamble. You are more likely to do that if replacement costs are low.

Shop-bought terminal rig, snooded hooks and sinker could easily cost £1 a throw, half of it on lead. Assuming you lose 6 sets of tackle a day—by no means excessive—the £3 worth of lost sinkers is equivalent to a boxful of home-made sinkers. Doing it yourself (make your own weights, tie snoods, cut down on swivels) slashes outlay to a few pence. Losing 10 rigs a day is of no consequence. Think how many more fish you would catch compared to the angler who is terrified of sacrificing his precious stock of 3 sinkers.

Moulding is the only way to be sure of the exact weight and shape of sinker best suited to your style of casting and fishing. Tackle shops tend to steer a middle course. They stock, say, 4, 5, 6 and 8 ounce weights, either plain bombs or Breakaways. American dealers prefer pyramids and bank sinkers. What if you need a 5.25, 5.5, 7, or 10 ounce weight? A long-tailed sinker instead of a squat bomb? You won't find one; it is as simple as that. The tackle trade is generally miles behind beach trends and developments. Thousands of British anglers use tournament-grade 150 gram sinkers. Not one shopkeeper in a hundred has even heard of them.

A note of caution

Sinker moulding is dangerous without strict safety rules. Very few serious accidents occur, but inexperienced fishermen burn their fingers or scare themselves silly. All but a handful of mishaps are the direct result of ignorance. It does not require genius to melt and mould scrap lead, but it is absolutely essential to follow a code of practice. The golden rule is NEVER POUR MOLTEN LEAD INTO A COLD, DAMP MOULD.

Hot lead instantly vapourises water. Steam expands . . . and literally explodes from the mould, blasting out a shower of metal. If you are looking down on the mould, the discharge hits you in the face and eyes. At best hot metal pours over your hands and clothing.

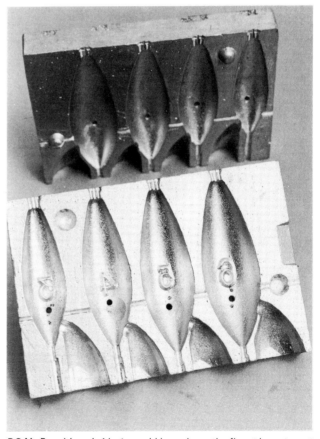

DCA's Beachbomb 4 in 1 mould is perhaps the finest investment for sinker making. Easy to use, accurate and safe, the four cavity mould produces conventional and long-tail sinkers.

Simple rules for handling molten lead:

1) Pre-heat the mould to warm it up and drive out dampness before you pour the first sinker.

2) Heat lead to well above melting point. Hot lead is easier to pour and runs cleanly into the depths of a mould. Semi-melted lead solidifies in the pouring hole and splashes on to the floor.

3) Make sure that the melting pot and boiler are secure. It is no fun tipping 10 pounds of molten lead over your toes. Moulds should be clamped if necessary, and laid on a flat surface. A tray of *dry* sand is an excellent base.

4) Use insulated gloves. Handle a very hot mould with pliers or clamps. Wear safety goggles and look away from the mould as the lead pours in.

5) NEVER COOL A MOULD IN WATER. This is the cardinal sin responsible for most serious accidents. Immersion inevitably results in a wet mould cavity. Pour molten lead inside that and you are in big trouble.

6) Pre-cut scrap chunks, make up wire loops beforehand and work to a pattern. A simple production sequence is faster and safer than flitting from one job to another.

7) Don't set the world on fire.

8) Lead poisoning. Metallic lead is unlikely to cause any problems. Bearing in mind the limited time spent in lead moulding and the low toxicity of clean scrap metal, an amateur who makes a few dozen sinkers now and again is perfectly safe provided he works in a well ventilated atmosphere.

Most lead poisoning is caused by fumes from lead-based chemicals like paint and organic compounds. There is more risk in burning off old lead paint than in melting scrap metal. Take care if your scrap is painted or corroded. Work in the open and avoid breathing the smoke. However, the risks are minimal—less than the intake of lead from petrol engine exhausts. But if you go on to make sinkers for friends and the local tackle shop, think about proper ventilation and regular health checks.

Moulds

Dozens of moulds are available from tackle shops and by mail order. Pyramids, grip leads and old-fashioned bombs in the 2–8 ounce range still grab a share of the market, but over the past 3 or 4 years new surf designs have infiltrated the home workshop. Aerodynamically superior bombs dominate tournament casting and top level beach fishing. Of the many moulds available, the DCA range are unquestionably best in both design and quality.

The Aquapedo bomb is short and fat, square in cross section and available in a 3–8 ounce range of 1 ounce increments. The sinker can be made up as a plain bomb, nose-wired sinker or collapsible wire version. Use either a short tail loop or a 3–4 inch single attachment wire. Aquapedoes are single cavity, die-cast moulds with a superb finish. The sections of mould are an absolutely immaculate fit, and no afterwork is necessary other than to trim off at the pouring gate. A snip with tin cutters produces the perfect sinker.

Beachbomb and Aquazoom sinkers are medium and long body sinkers respectively. The Beachbomb is shaped like an elongated tear drop, neatly pointed back and front, and with a centre of gravity just forward of the halfway point. The cross section is round. Aquazooms are longer, slimmer, and polygonal in cross section. Like Aquapedoes they may be assembled in plain and wired form with short loops or long tails. Beachbombs are particularly good for conversion into Spanish-style long tailed casting sinkers.

The range of sizes expands in step with modern thinking. The 3–10 ounce range is adequately covered, and there is a special 150 gram version of both sinkers. The Aquazoom 150 gram has been chosen as our official tournament casting sinker. Moulds are produced with double and multiple cavities. The 3, 4, 5, 6 ounce 4 in 1 Beachbomb unit is excellent—good value for money, easy to use, accurate and covers every basic requirement of beach fishing.

Glynn and Michael Williams of DCA moulds are sometimes willing to make up special designs and sizes to order. However, as the standard range continues to expand this service is largely unnecessary. If you cannot find a DCA mould to suit, you must be very fussy indeed. Most good tackle shops stock them. In case of difficulty—and for export sales—contact DCA Moulds, 41 Lon Isa, Rhiwbina, Cardiff, CF4 6EE, WALES, Great Britain. Telephone 0222 65340. Prices range from around £4 for a single cavity mould to £8 for a 4 in 1 Beachbomb outfit.

Other moulds exist of course. Some manufacturers offer a reasonable product at respectable prices, so do not despair if you cannot find a genuine DCA mould. The difference between the majority of mould makers and the Williams team is that Glynn and Michael regard sinkers as technical products worthy of deep research and high quality engineering, not as chunks of boiled scrap lead.

Lead

Fifteen pounds of scrap lead should last most beach fishermen a year or more. That much can usually be scrounged from somewhere: demolition sites, ripped out plumbing, ancient drainpipes. If all else fails, buy clean scrap from your local metal dealer. Even at full price it is far cheaper than ready-made sinkers.

Lead varies in weight and texture. Pure lead is heavy but soft. Scrap wheel balance weights are harder but weigh less. Mix them together if you like. Using several different batches of scrap metal in a nominal 5 ounce mould, the sinkers turn out between 4.75 and 5.25 ounces—accurate enough for most purposes.

Clean sheet lead is easiest to work with. Raw scrap is dirty, painted, corroded, in pipe form or in crunched blocks. Scrape off the worst muck and carve the lead into manageable pieces with an old axe, metal shears or by hammer and cold chisel. Aim for a piece of lead which can be lowered straight into the melting pot.

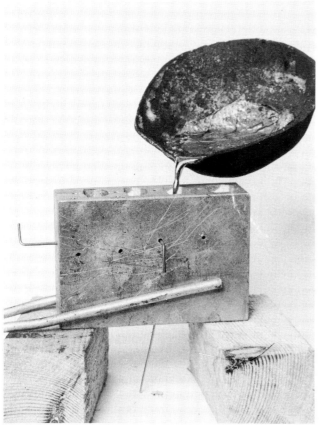

The mould set up for lead pouring. The halves are securely clamped and rested on blocks of wood which allow clearance for the long tail wire. Angled brass wires form tunnels in the lead for sinker wire attachment.

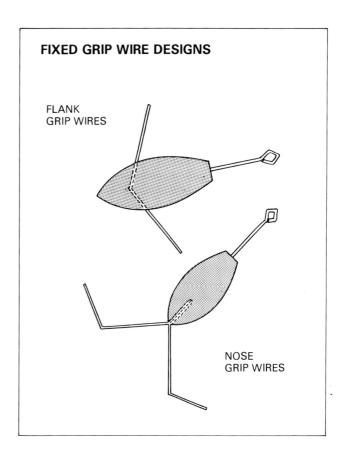

FIXED GRIP WIRE DESIGNS

FLANK
GRIP WIRES

NOSE
GRIP WIRES

Wires

Stainless steel, galvanised and brass wire loops link the sinker to its trace. All three are satisfactory but stainless steel is best in the long run. Loops must seat deeply inside the lead for security. Cut off 3 inches of wire, bend it into a 'U' the same width as the mould channels, then fold over the last 0.25 inch of each free end. Even small tags of metal will handle 8–10 ounce weights without slipping out in mid-cast. Long tail wires must be made from stainless steel wire. Cut 5–6 inch pieces of wire, fold the last 0.5 inch of one end into a 'U' and insert it about an inch into the mould cavity.

Grip wires are best cut from springy stainless steel wire. Failing that, piano wire will do despite the rust. Brass and galvanised steel are usually too soft to bother with; thicker wire works well enough, but creates so much air resistance that casts are noticeably reduced. For nose wires, cut a pair of 7–8 inch wires, fold them in half and insert the hinged ends about 0.5 inches into the mould. Fixed flank wires are cut to the same length but bent into right-angles for mounting in the mould holes.

Wire specifications

Tackle dealers sell wire by the yard or metre. Metal stockists prefer to sell by weight—usually one kilogramme minimum order. There is no precise diameter and grade of wire best suited to sinker production but do choose fairly springy wire that is easy to cut and bend.

79

Purpose	S.W.G.	Diameter	U.S. equivalent (Brown and Sharpe)
Heavy	14	0.080″/2.03mm	No. 12
General	16	0.064″/1.625mm	No. 14
Light	18	0.048″/1.219 mm	No. 16

General purpose wire suits 4–8 ounce sinkers with grips up to 4 inches long and short or long tail loops.

Heavy wire encourages firm anchorage in very fast tides. Wires can be extended to 6–8 inches if necessary. Extra strength is some insurance against snapping off 8–12 ounce sinkers cast very hard, and is mandatory for 14–16 ounces of lead.

Light wire is of limited usefulness in surf fishing. Sinkers up to 3 ounces are safely cast on 18SWG loops. For the long tail design, stick to 16SWG wire when hard casting cannot be avoided.

Pre-formed loops
DAC Moulds produce a range of brass and galvanised steel tail loops which slot into the mould. Unlike ordinary loops, Aqualoops can be inserted after the mould is closed and clamped. Instead of having metal tags at the end of the 'U' piece, Aqualoops are corrugated for most of their length. The arrangement seems flimsy but it works extremely well. 8 ounces of lead cast at full power are perfectly secure. However, lead must be poured red hot otherwise it does not run into close enough contact with the wire to infiltrate the corrugations.

Tools and equipment
Asbestos gloves
Blowtorch to melt lead and pre-heat the mould
Container to hold molten lead
Pouring ladle
Wire cutters and pliers
Sand tray
Clamps
Old knife to trim sinkers
Rubber bands for collapsible sinkers (optional)
Fire bricks to reflect and conserve blowtorch heat
Secure stand for lead pot and ladle

Over the years my sinker moulding equipment and technique have evolved into a streamlined production system. Once it took an hour to set up the heater and melt the first batch of lead. Now I make a dozen weights in 30 minutes.

The traditional way of handling lead is to melt it in an iron pot heated by a gas ring or brazier.

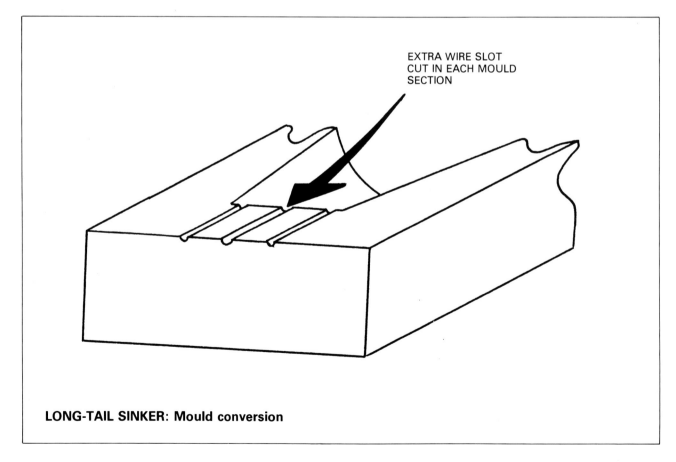

EXTRA WIRE SLOT CUT IN EACH MOULD SECTION

LONG-TAIL SINKER: Mould conversion

handle the hot mould with insulated gloves or pliers. The 5 ounce sinker shown here is ready for trimming. Note the brass wire used to pre-drill the sinker body.

Work with 5–10 pounds of lead at once, and skim off dross which rises to the surface. Heat the ladle, fill it from the melting pot, then pour the sinker. Nothing wrong in doing it that way, except that it swallows up too much time and heat. Besides you need a proper gas ring which securely supports the lead pot, a separate ladle, and a lot of fuel to first break down that great chunk of lead and then keep it molten. It takes as much heat to maintain molten metal as it does to melt it in the first place.

I now use a powerful propane blowtorch (butane is just as good) aimed directly on to a lead ladle. The ladle is either hand held over the flame or steadied in a cradle of fire bricks surrounding the burner nozzle. Instead of melting several pounds of lead, I use enough for, say, 4 sinkers at once. Using a pair of double-cavity moulds or a set of individuals, I can set up the moulds and wires, melt lead and pour the whole lot in one go. Molten metal runs out from under the dross, so there is seldom any reason to skim the surface beforehand.

Any safe method is acceptable, and with experience you soon develop your own particular way of working. Full-scale production does require a lot of thought and plenty of equipment, but at the other extreme plenty of anglers knock out

enough sinkers for their own use by melting lead in an old saucepan on the kitchen range. Gas cookers and electric radiant rings make short work of scrap lead.

Systematic working reduces waste, speeds production and is safer. The method detailed here is by no means the only one, and perhaps not even the best. However, it is both easy and safe—prime considerations for a beginner.

1) Work outside or in your garage. Use the floor rather than a bench. That way, spilled lead splashes less. Plain concrete is best. Avoid combustible dust and wood shavings!

2) Set up your mould with wires in place, halves firmly clamped together and the whole thing set firmly on a sand tray or supported on bricks. (Sometimes the mould must be held high because there are wires dangling below.)

3) Arrange 4 or 5 fire bricks in an open square: 2 for the base, 3 for the sides. Turn on the blowtorch and rest its nozzle on the brick floor with the flame directed into the box. Drop a chunk of lead into the ladle and melt it. Either hold the

81

ladle or make up a simple iron stand for it. I hold mine because I find it easier to work that way. I use insulated gloves all the time though; some people find them a nuisance.

4) When the lead is nicely melted, pick up the blowtorch and cook the mould for a minute to drive out moisture and to ensure that lead does not harden in the pouring hole. By this time the lead in the ladle has cooled a little but it takes only a minute's more heating to bring it back to optimum working temperature.

5) Pour lead steadily into the mould until it overflows into the pouring hole. If you are working with more than one mould, fill them in turn. Warm the ladle between pourings. The hotter the lead, the smoother and shinier the sinker will turn out.

6) Rest your ladle somewhere safe—it should now be empty or almost so—and turn off the gas. Lead sets within 30 seconds, so it is already time to split the mould. Remove clamps and open the

mould halves with gloved fingers (carefully!) or with pliers.

If necessary, first remove the anchor wire guide pins from their holes. These are brass wires one size thicker than stainless wire used for grips. Slide them into the access holes in the mould, pour the lead, then pull them out to produce a pair of neat tunnels through the sinker body.

7) Knock the sinker from its mould and leave it to cool. At this stage it is safe to drop just the sinker into water. NEVER SOAK THE MOULD. Finally, insert new tail loops and wires, close the mould and clamp it. Melt more lead for the next batch of sinkers. It is no longer necessary to preheat the moulds. By the second pouring most moulds are throughly hot; after moulding 3 or 4 sinkers they are too hot to handle even with gloves.

AFTERWORK

Plain sinkers

Trim off excess lead and clean out the tail wire loop. Check loop security. There is no need to pull

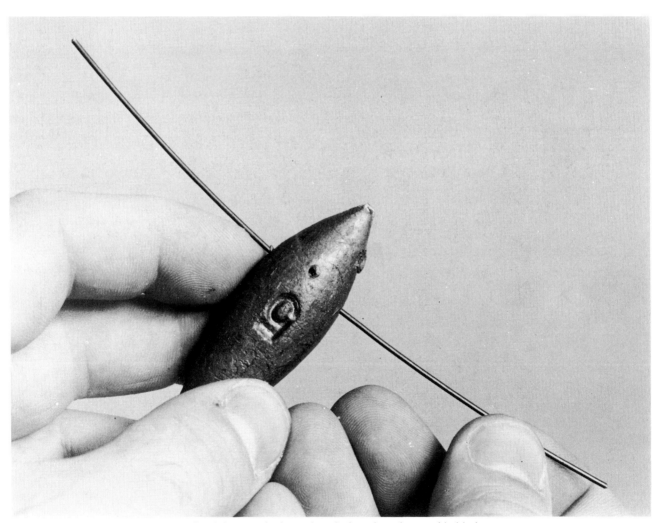

Grip wires 1. Cut two 9 inch pieces of stainless steel wire and push them into the moulded holes.

Grip wires 2. Centre the wires in their holes, then bend the ends over.

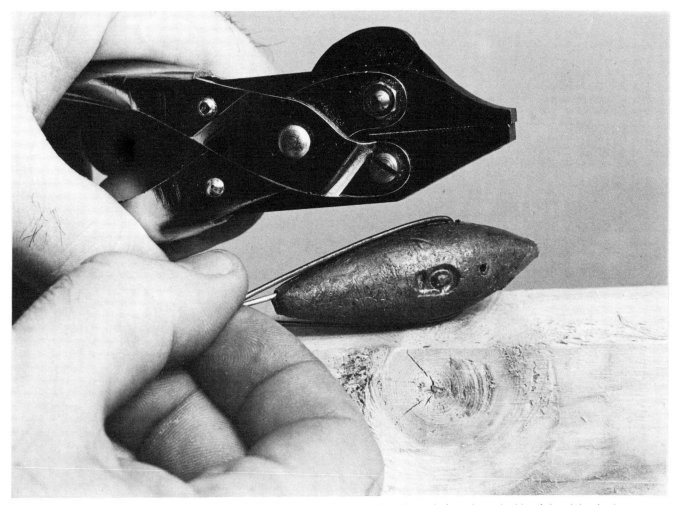

Grip wires 3. Lay the sinker on a block of soft wood and tap the wire so that channels form in each side of the sinker body.

Grip wires 4. *Allow an inch of wire to lay along the sinker flank. Bend the rest outwards by 45 degrees.*

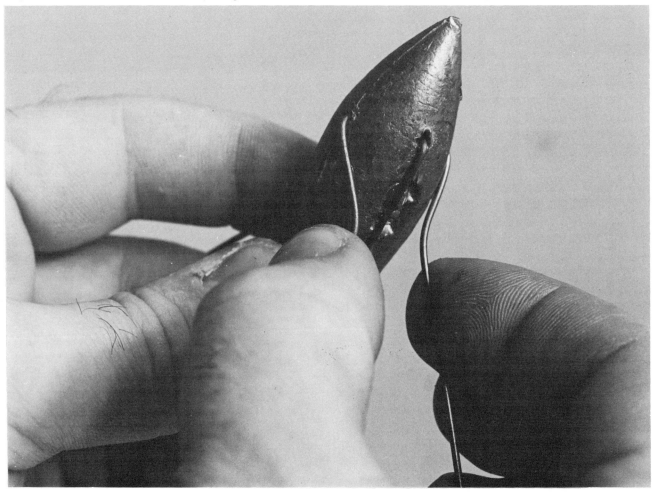

Grip wires 5. *Bend the wires inward so that they slot tightly into the sinker body channels. Wire tension determines the line pressure at which the wires flip from the seabed.*

hard. Unless the wire loops has shifted in the mould and now pokes out of the lead body, it will be safely attached. Aqualoops should be tested by pulling on the tail with pliers—use about 50 pounds pressure. This test confirms that molten lead has set in close contact with the serrated wire. The final test is to weigh the sinker. Unnecessary for general fishing, it is a valuable step for tournament casters. There is no point practising with a 5 ounce sinker if 5.25 ounces are standard for the event.

Grip-wired sinkers

No extra work is involved if wires are permanently fixed inside a lead body. Nose and flank wires should be cleaned of lead flashing and stray blobs. Sometimes excess lead must be pared away before the mould halves will separate. Store the sinkers with nose wires left straight and flank wires folded against the body. Just before use, bend the wires into grapnel pattern. Wire angle depends on the seabed and tide flow. Hard tides and sand/grit require steeply raked wires. Soft mud or a gentle flow are better handled with reduced gripping power, so spread the wires well away from the lead. For even more grip in adverse conditions, form a shallow hook in the last inch of each grapnel finger.

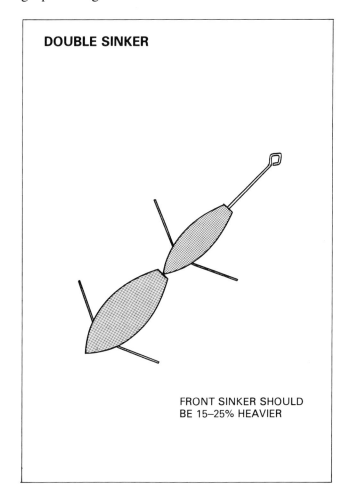

DOUBLE SINKER

FRONT SINKER SHOULD
BE 15–25% HEAVIER

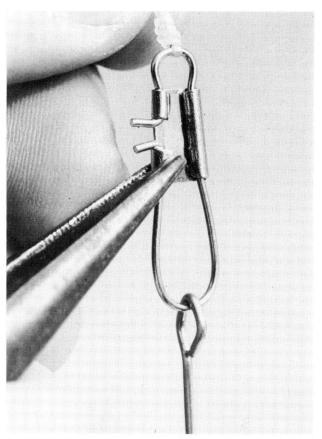

Conventional clips and split rings are perfectly safe provided the design is right. Safety pin clips like this tend to open under pressure. Nip the tag of metal to lock the wire in place. Note the open diamond loop in the tail wire.

Collapsible or breakaway wires are threaded through holes moulded into the sinker, bent into shape and held in position by rubber bands or wire tension. Wire tension is a better system because there are no bands to snap. The picture sequence shows exactly how to make a Breakaway, perhaps the most versatile sinker ever developed for surf fishing.

Mould modifications

DCA moulds are available pre-drilled for grip wires either in the nose, fixed in the flank or swivelling. Other moulds are easily drilled to take either anchor wires or brass guide pins. Drill the holes one size larger than anchor wire diameter. For accurate hole alignment across the halves of the mould, mark the drilling positions before hand, and bore each half of the mould separately from inside the cavity.

Some moulds are predrilled for conventional and single-tail wires. Others are slotted for the loop only. Three or four strokes of a sharp hacksaw in each half of the mould produce a neat central tail hole into which you insert a single wire. Long tail wires have many advantages over the short loop. They cast smoothly and perhaps a little farther than the regular design; seabed anchorage is at least 30 percent higher.

Double sinkers

An additional advantage of the long single tail wire is that two lead bodies, each with grip wires, can be moulded one behind the other. Use your normal 3–6 ounce moulds to produce double sinkers between 6 and 12 ounces. It pays to use sinkers at least an ounce different in weight, with the heavier body at the front. Short aerodynamic shapes are best, thus Beachbomb and Aquapedo moulds reign supreme. Armed with 10 ounces-plus of double bomb and two sets of grip wires, you can tackle the heaviest seas with confidence.

Sleeve attachment 1. Bend a tight "U" in the wire. Tie the leader directly to the wire with a Uni-knot.

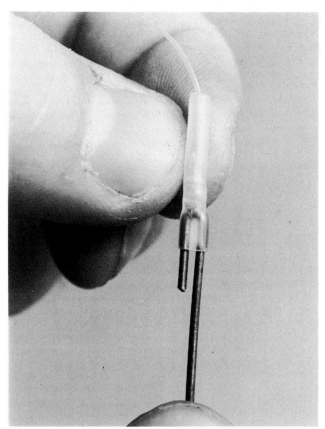

Sleeve attachment 2. Protect the knot and close the wire bend with a piece of tight fitting plastic tube. This is a cheap and highly effective way to secure a surfcasting sinker.

Hooks

Hooks are used to present baits and trap biting fish; that much holds true for any kind of fishing. Casting from the shore presents its own difficulties, most of them related to long distance. Hooks which control baits and hook fish at 50 yards may prove useless at 100 yards. Beyond 150 yards it is extremely difficult to catch fish at all unless your hooks are close to perfect.

The first hurdle is bait preservation. Does the worm, fish strip or peeler crab stay on the hook, or does it explode in mid-cast? If a cast holds together, does the weight of the hook upset a bait's action underwater? Some fish ignore a piece of worm anchored by thick stainless steel but will snatch the same bait threaded on narrow gauge wire.

The teeth of rays, smoothhounds and dogfish are flat and strong. Powered by massive grinding muscles capable of pulverising shellfish and hard crabs, a big fish's jaws literally crush medium-weight hooks. Fine-wire Aberdeen hooks used extensively in match fishing last but a few seconds.

Tope and conger eels crush and cut their prey. A strong hook is essential, and this time it needs the support of a wire trace. However, a substantial hook is no good unless razor sharp—tope, especially, are hard to hook at long range. Conger are a short to medium range species, but they too require a fair impact to sink the barb. Blunt hooks skid off their rubbery jaws.

There are fish that suck and nibble a bait, and some that swallow whole. Short shank hooks are good enough for wide-throated species which can be unhooked with forceps or pliers. Long shank hooks are better for flatfish and other narrow jawed fish which swallow a hook right down; you can still reach the end of the shank for unhooking. Sometimes it pays to tie on a fine wire hook which can be deliberately pulled straight. There is no easier and kinder way to unhook a deeply impaled flounder, sole or dab.

Tying and whipping, snood modification and bait clips contribute to better casting and bait protection. Simple alterations in hook design and size make life a lot easier on the beach. One problem remains: how to drive home a hook at long range. Striking is useless. At even 75 yards a powerful sweep of the rod shifts the hook only a few inches and generates a point pressure of less than 12 ounces.

Special traces and grip wire sinker allow us to reverse the process so that the fish hooks itself, but it can do so only if the hook is sharp, easily sunk beyond barb depth and capable of taking a firm grip in soft tissues as well as hard. The right choice of hook turns 9 bites out of 10 into hooked fish. The wrong one is a total failure.

No hook is beyond criticism. There are plenty of really bad ones, half a dozen which excel, and a reasonable selection of middle of the road designs which are neither atrocious nor inspiring. And to be truly successful any hook must be chosen in relation to a *combination* of bait size, casting range, species, hooking power and strength. Compromise is usually necessary, and for that reason alone very few anglers are without their individual preferences. However, there is a broad consensus about the hooks that are worth buying and those which are completely useless. Very few match fishermen would use the sliced beaked design, but everyone would have a few blue Aberdeens in his bag.

PATTERNS, SIZES AND APPLICATIONS

Fine wire Blue Aberdeens

These are something of a cult hook. Extremely sharp, thin in the wire and modestly strong, they are *the* hook for small fish and delicate baits. Long range fishing for dabs, pouting, whiting and even shy codling is enhanced by a blue Aberdeen. Smaller sizes—size 6 to 1/0— are used all around the British coast for competition work and general pleasure fishing. Some anglers take the view that unless you are fishing specifically for big cod, conger or rays, there is really no need to use any other design of saltwater hook. There are several types of Aberdeen hook, many of which are available in blued steel. The one usually referred to as a genuine Aberdeen Blue is the plain shank (no ring or spade) Mustad 3730A. Aberdeen Blues can be pulled from a fish's throat and re-bent into shape, a most useful trick in high-speed match fishing.

Ringed Aberdeen hooks

These offer improved strength at the slight sacrifice of sharpness and penetration. They are stocked by most dealers and commonly available in the size 6–8/0 range, which covers every

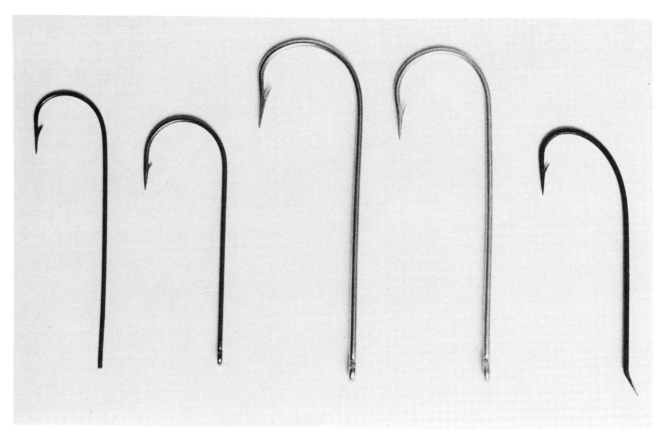

Lightweight shore hooks. Right to left: Breakaway Spearspade, Au Lion d'Or 1322, Mustad Aberdeen 3282, Partridge Aberdeen Z10, and the classic blue Aberdeen 3730A from Mustad.

requirement. Above all they are an excellent general purpose hook for worm presentation, sandeels and fish strips. Whiting, flatfish, bass and cod are hooked and held without much risk of struggling free. Be careful of hauling heavy fish through strong surf—there is a limit to the insurance provided by the relatively slim, modestly tempered wire. Mustad 3282 are popular, usually in silver and with neat eyes for direct trace attachment.

Au Lion d'Or (model 1322) hooks from France are similar to the Mustad Aberdeen. The wire is slightly thicker and much tougher, making the larger sizes a particularly wise choice for winter cod. Few shops have them in stock. The finish looks like satin chrome; whatever it is, the hook is fairly stain resistant and can be used several times before rust sets in.

The sharpest, strongest and best tempered Aberdeen is made by Partridge of Redditch, England. Most sizes are available, and as the hook gains popularity because of its sheer quality, more and more tackle shops sell them. The model number is Z10, sizes 8 to 4/0. A shorter shank version is available under code Z9A in sizes 6 to 3/0. Both models are bronzed and eyed. Patridge have recently introduced a blue steel Aberdeen, Z12, which is lighter than the Z10, plain shanked and sized 8 to 4/0. Quality, temper and sharpness

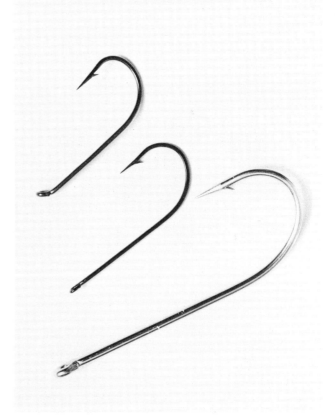

Strong and medium weight hooks for shore fishing. Right to left: Partridge, Kendal, Kirby, Extra-strong (Z22), Mustad Viking 79515 and Partridge Flashpoint Z5.

88

are higher than Mustad's blue Aberdeen—the two brands are set for major confrontation in the sea match world.

Mustad Viking, Spearspade, Spearpoint and Patridge Flashpoint

These hooks lie midway between the delicate accuracy of Aberdeens and the large, rugged sea hooks which are all power and no finesse. There is no reason why any of these models should not be substituted for Aberdeens except for fishing fragile baits like white ragworm.

Mustad Vikings are produced in a number of basically similar models. Numbers 79510 and 79515, its successor, are classic hooks for big cod and bass. Forged, well tempered, sharp and medium-weight in the wire, they accept bunches of worms, squid and whole crabs with ease. Many sizes are available, and the most popular lie between size 2 and 4/0.

Breakaway Tackle's Spearpoint and Spearspade hooks are manufactured by Patridge. Essentially the same hook with either a small eye or extended spade, they are offspring of traditional low-water salmon hooks. Needle sharpness and high strength in relation to wire diameter are two key features of the range. Rather than rely on size numbers alone, Breakaway Tackle grade their hooks according to species: cod, bass, whiting and dab. Beginners particularly welcome the neat packaging which carries tying instructions and selection guide.

Many cod anglers believe that an extended shank promotes better long-range hooking. Breakaway and Vikings are borderline in this respect, and thus rejected by a section of the cod fishing community. Patridge offer a reasonable alternative in the Z5 Flashpoint series, sizes 6 to 7/0. Bronzed, forged hooks with round bend and small turned-down eyes, they are exceedingly sharp and adequately tough.

An appropriately sized hook from this group will handle the majority of baits used from the surf and should easily land most species of fish from dabs and soles, through codling, dogfish and bass, right up to medium-weight rays, tope and conger eels.

Heavy duty hooks

These are seldom strictly necessary for British surf fishing but may prove essential for overseas sport. Mustad produce a vast array of models and sizes. O'Shaughnessy and Seamaster are fine examples. Closer to home, the Partridge Kendal Kirby Extra Strong (Z22) is well worth considering. Scalpel-sharp point, round, offset bend and realistically slim, nickel plated shank are a challenge to any

tope and conger eel. Were it exported to America, drum and striper fishermen might find it a realistic alternative to the standard surf hooks. Penetration is markedly superior to most large hooks—a tremendous advantage with hard-mouthed species at medium to long range.

Do you really need a big strong hook? This depends on where you fish and the chances of hooking a monster. In general, surf fishermen underrate their tackle. Small hooks are not necessarily inferior; and there is some truth in the theory that hook size and power should be reduced to match main line and trace breaking strains. Why use a hook of 300 pounds breaking strain on 20 pound test tackle?

Hooks are subject to enormous leverage and crushing pressures. It is unrealistic to expect a weak hook to deal with very big, hard fighting fish. However, sometimes the size of a hook is its own worst enemy. Angles of barb, point and shank, bend circumference and wire diameter sometimes make it easier for a big fish to break away from or even straighten a large hook. Small hooks—provided they are reasonably strong in the wire and well made—sink in much deeper, so that fighting stress is transferred from the point to the back of the bend, a far more solid foundation.

Tests suggest that a small hook set deep is much more reliable and actually stronger than a big hook

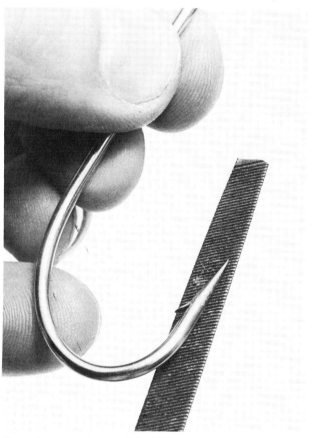

Sharp hooks catch more fish. A file or slip stone soon corrects blunt points caused by sand and stones.

Snelling 1. Fold a loop about six inches in diameter and lay it alongside the hook shank.

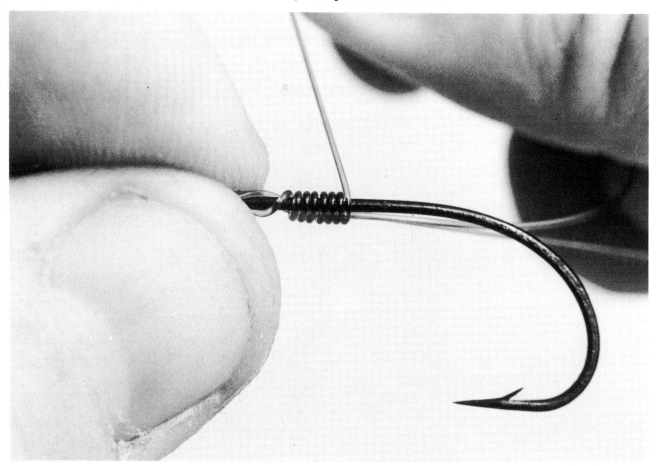

Snelling 2. Hold the left hand end of the loop between right finger and thumb, and whip it neatly around the shank and double strands of nylon. Put in at least six full turns.

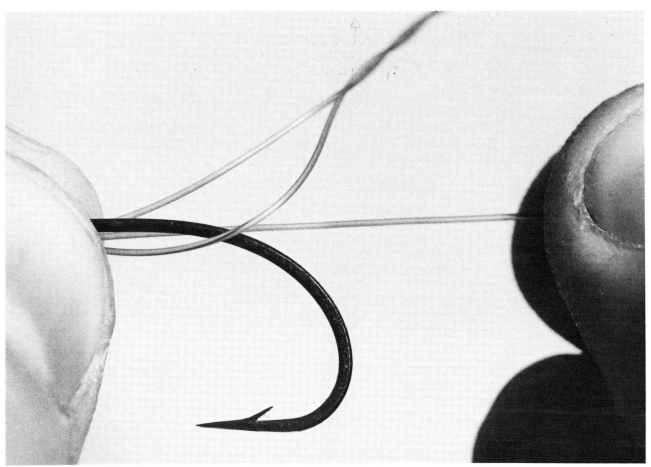

Snelling 3. *Carefully slide your left finger and thumb over the coils and pinch them to the shank. Now pull on the spare end of nylon to tighten the knot.*

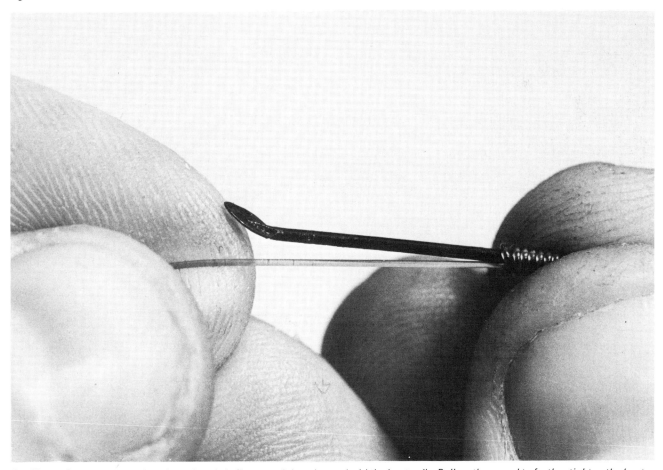

Snelling 4. *Swap over your hands so that right finger and thumb now hold the knot coils. Pull on the snood to further tighten the knot.*

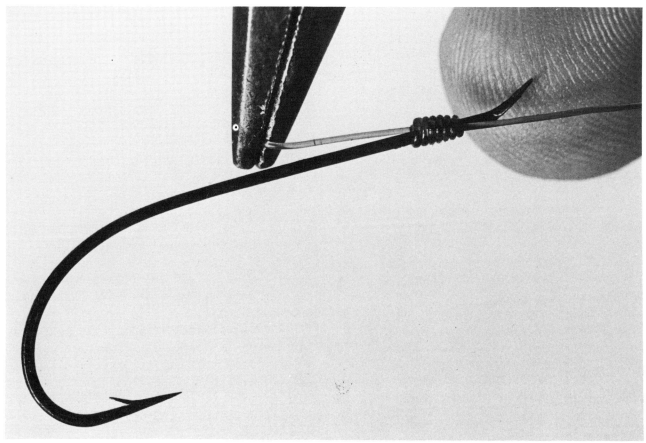

Snelling 5. *Slide the knot close to the spade end. Pull the knot tight with pliers. Finally trim the loose end.*

sunk only to barb depth. There is another factor: hooks affect a bait's action on the seabed. Instead of rolling with the current, baits on big, coarse hooks hold fast in the sand by the sheer weight of the hook. Some fish are not concerned with the unnatural reaction; others swim right past. If everyone around you is catching fish while your bait lies ignored, try changing to a smaller or lighter hook. Hook weight is more deterring than an exposed shank.

Hook attachment

Hooks are manufactured with plain shanks, eyes and spade-end tags. Sometimes there is no apparent balance between hook design and attachment system—hooks are for the most part the result of traditional craftsmanship. Anglers too have their preferences: some match anglers insist on a spade end while others choose the same hook with an eye. There are definite advantages in spades and plain shanks, but for beginners the eyed hook is best because it is so easy to tie to the trace. Whipping and snelling are more demanding, and in many cases the extra work is hardly justified for general fishing.

Whipped hooks

A fine wire, needle sharp Aberdeen Blue supports the most fragile worm bait. The delicate white

ragworm loses only a drop of blood when the point and barb are inserted. A whole worm threads neatly up the shank and on to the trace. Hardly damaged by the hooking process, it casts well and retains all its attractive juices.

The same worm slips neatly on to an ordinary eyed Aberdeen or Viking hook, threads smoothly on to the shank, then stops fast against the eye and knot. The smallest eye effectively trebles shank diameter, and worms cannot be threaded on to the trace without splitting the body wide open. Blood and juices are lost; the bait explodes in mid-cast.

Aberdeen Blues are super-glued and whipped so neatly to the trace that a worm's body hardly expands as it slides into position. There is no particular skill in whipping plain shanked hooks, but it is not easy to produce a reliable bond between shank and trace unless you work carefully. No matter how tightly you whip, thread tension alone will not anchor the components. Nylon and metal must first be bonded, then whipped, and finally sealed. Try this technique (see the photographs for close-up details):

1) Clean the hook shank with methylated spirit to remove grease. Spread a thin smear of superglue along the back of the shank. Lay on a nylon snood and hold the two in close contact until the glue sets.

92

2) Trim off the nylon with a sloping cut and whip it to the shank with medium weight Gudebrod rod thread. Tie off the whipping with the normal rod maker's tuck. Check the alignment of snood and shank and adjust if necessary. They must lie parallel.

3) Smear superglue over the entire whipping and leave it to dry. Adhesive seeps into the threads and fuses shank, thread and nylon into one smooth layer. Because of the sloping cut made in the nylon, the whipping is nicely tapered for easy bait threading. After a few hours' drying the hook is ready to use.

Superglue is not waterproof. In time, saltwater eats into the whipping and breaks the bond. This is seldom a problem in everyday beach fishing; hooks never last that long. It is possible for hooks stored in a damp tin to gradually lose strength, so if you go fishing infrequently, add a smear of varnish to the whipping for extra protection. Do not take chances: good whippings are as strong as eyes and spades, but bad ones are the worst possible way to attach hooks to snoods.

Ordinary Aberdeens and some lightweight Vikings and Spearpoints may be whipped. Cut off the eye or spade and use the standard whipping technique after cleaning the shank and perhaps roughening it slightly with a file for a better key. Take care when trimming the hook shank. Snipping off with pliers produces a sharp edge which would cut the snood. Grind the end of the wire square across on a slipstone.

Best results are ensured by matching hook wire to nylon snood diameter. They should be fairly similar otherwise either the snood slides out or the hook pulls from under its tube of whipping. Matt-finish brands of monofilament like Sylcast and Stren bond better than shiny, cheap lines. If necessary though you can key the nylon by gently pulling it through folded abrasive paper.

Eyed hooks
Eyes are an excellent link between hook shank and trace. Nothing is easier to tie or more reliable. Where tackle strength outweighs bait disruption, an eyed shank outfishes every other hook. Several knots may be used, and with wire traces you have the choice between tying, twisting and crimping.

There are anglers who spend hours experimenting with knots. According to them, certain knots are superior in terms of impact resistance and overall strength. They can show you clear evidence that a tucked blood knot is far from the ideal choice. That may be so in the laboratory, and might even prove correct in ideal fishing conditions. Given warm, dry hands, plenty of time to retie if necessary and perfect lighting, anyone can learn to make those complicated super-knots so often written about yet so seldom used.

Icy fingers, slippery tackle and no time for hesitation are another matter. Then it pays to tie the good old tucked blood knot, Uni-knot or Palomar. It is better to hit the target every time with a 80-90 percent strength knot than to struggle with that elusive 99 percent hitch that goes wrong four times out of five. After practising for 10 minutes, most beginners can tie simpler knots reliably. Coils snug down neatly, and the knot stays firm under pressure. If you tie 6 tucked blood knots and test each for strength, each one's breaking point should be within 5 or 10 percent of maximum value.

Palomars and Uni-knots show a similar pattern. But 6 examples of a more critical knot might test out this way: 95 percent, 97, 95, 55, 90 and 70. If all goes well, the knot is indeed superior. Now and again it falls flat; in accordance with Murphy's Law, that's the time you will hook a king-size bass or cod.

The tucked half blood knot is good enough for general fishing. Better still, use the Uni-knot which

Small fish are an important part of modern shore fishing. It pays to scale down your hooks accordingly.

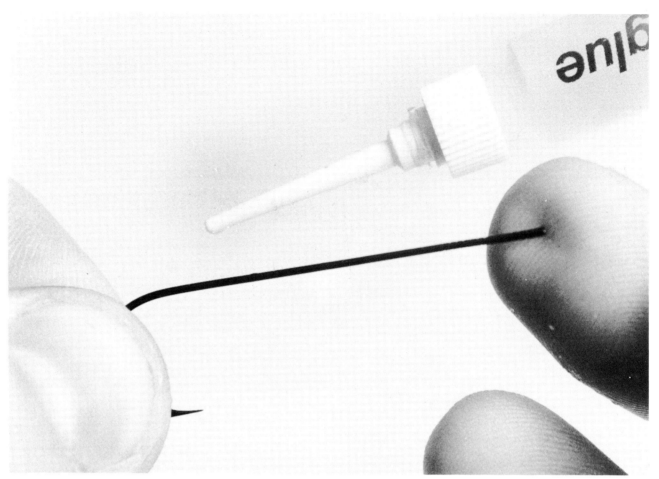

Whipping 1. *Smear superglue down the shank. If necessary, first clean the wire with methylated spirit or Ajax.*

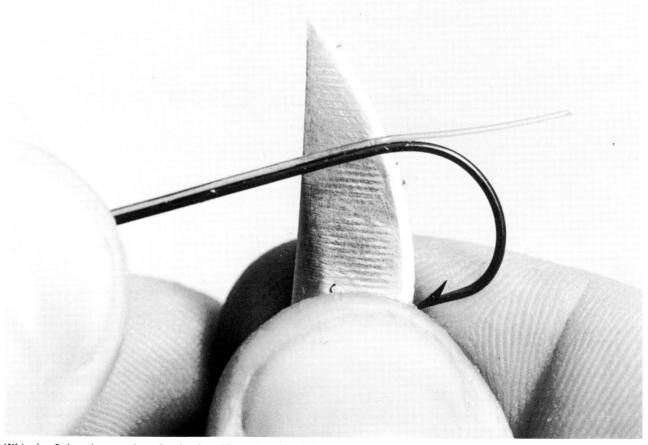

Whipping 2. *Lay the snood on the shank and leave it to bond. Trim the end of nylon close to the bend with a tapering cut.*

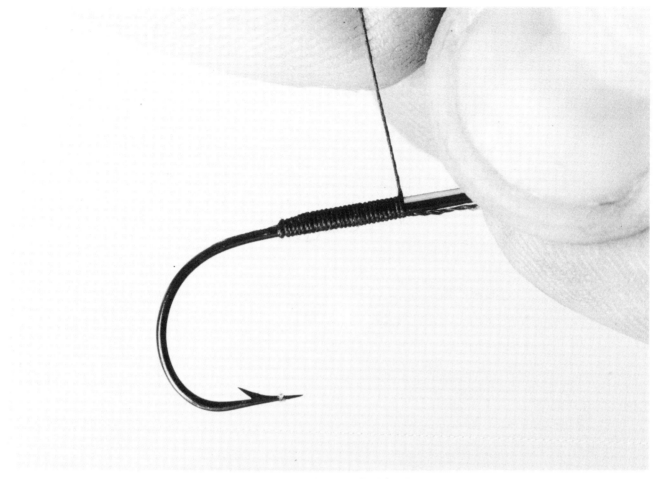

Whipping 3. *Begin whipping the shank with ordinary sewing thread or Budebrod rod thread.*

Whipping 4. *Tie off the thread with the normal rod maker's tuck.*

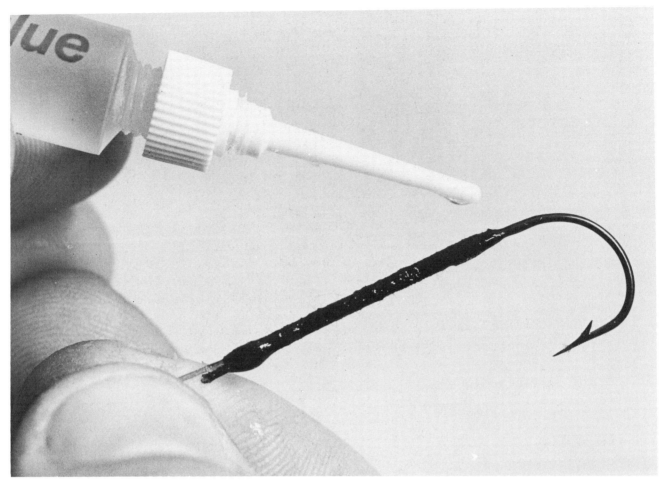

Whipping 5. Adjust the shank and snood so they lie parallel, then seal the threads with superglue.

is slightly stronger provided the coils fall neatly into place. A little practice develops the skill necessary to tie the knot with your eyes closed. Make sure the coils align correctly *before* you tighten the knot, otherwise they ride over each other and skid free. The Palomar also depends on sensible practice and care in smoothing its parallel coils before you pull them tight. Its great advantage is the double run of nylon around the hook eye. The spare end of Uni-knots and Palomars lies parallel to the snood, whereas a sprig of nylon juts out at right-angles from the blood knot barrel. Mostly it makes no difference, but with soft worm baits the blood knot may cause some damage.

Snelled hooks
Spade end hooks are attached with a special snell which is easy to tie once you see it done, and on the whole makes a reasonably reliable, tough joint. A traditional favourite of commercial fishermen, the spade hook/snell combination is much faster to tie than a plain shank whipping (which can be used on a spade end hook if you prefer). Spade end hooks are cheaper than eyed models; looking at it the other way, only cheap hooks are spaded. Keen surf men steer clear.

I see little reason for snelled hooks in beach fishing. Either proper whippings or knotted eyes are much better. However, one advantage of the system is that it holds the hook shank straight out from the trace, whereas an eyed hook tends to fold. Sometimes bait presentation is enhanced by a straight joint, and in those circumstances a snell is preferred. Spade ends are not necessary; the hitch can be tied just as easily on an eyed hook. Either treat the eye as an ordinary spade, or thread line through beforehand. As long as the trace nylon is fairly thin, a snell will not damage threaded worms.

Looped-on hooks are a satisfactory means of baiting with sandeels and sprats. Tie a trace-end loop long enough to slide through the eye and around the hook bend. Push the loop into the eye, attach the bait, take the loop around the hook and bait; halfpay draw the loop into the eye. Tuck the fish's tail under the double strand, then pull the knot tight.

Hook modification
Cutting off eyes has already been discussed. It opens up the field for whipping stronger hooks than Aberdeen Blues. Why bother? It means you

can avoid bursting worms against the normal shank eye yet still choose a reasonably strong wire. At the same time you can modify shank length. Trimmed down by a few millimetres, long shank Aberdeens are more suited to short, bulky baits like crabs and shellfish.

An offset hook point definitely increases hooking power. Many otherwise excellent surf-casting hooks are manufactured with straight shanks only. If the wire is well forged and highly tempered, it is a mistake to offset the bend. Softer hooks are modified by a slight twist with pliers. It does not matter whether a bend is offset left or right.

You can take the process one stage further. If you think that a size 1 Aberdeen should be thicker in the wire, reform a smaller bend in a standard 2/0 hook. Some Aberdeens are soft enough for safe bending as long as you leave the point alone.

Hooks are usually over-long in point and barb. A minute's work with a file and slipstone reduces the metal and creates a much sharper, secure point. Patridge hooks never need this modification. One star attraction of the range is the excellent design of the sharp end.

Sharpening hooks
Again with the notable exception of Partridge and Breakaway, most of the world's surfcasting hooks are supplied relatively blunt, or at least subject to wide variation. Before using any hook, and from time to time while fishing, touch up the point with a file or slipstone. Absolute sharpness is difficult to maintain because of sand and stone abrasion.

An ideal hookpoint is chisel shaped and relatively short, not round and long like a needle. Short points last much longer, and they do not skid off or fold over anywhere near as easily when a fish bites. It takes but a few strokes of the file 3 or 4 times a day to keep your hook in perfect condition. A small price to pay for peace of mind and better sport.

Traces and Accessories

There are no world-wide standards for traces and terminal rigs. Every country develops its own themes. Fishermen 50 miles along the coast probably use a different rig from your own. Species and sea conditions, baits and tackle influence trace and accessory design. The seasons bring their own changes: a rig for summer fishing might be entirely useless on the same beach in January.

Experiment is the key to successful bait presentation. It really does pay to ring the changes with trace length and breaking strain, paternoster arrangement, sinker weight, hook size and how baits are cut. Sometimes bass ignore ragworms presented on paternoster snoods yet bite freely on a single hook rig allowed to wash over the seabed. Cod often take an opposite view: well anchored baits on short paternoster snoods attract five fish to the running leger's one.

Little can be predicted. Surf fishing changes from day to day, and sometimes morning tides fish differently from late evening tides. What a surf man needs above all is a sound background knowledge of how rigs work and how they are best constructed. Simplicity is the underlying theme.

Paternosters account for the vast majority of fish hooked in the surf, short range or at maximum distance. Paternosters are easy to tie, versatile and they definitely reduce bait explosion. Set properly in the tide, a paternoster virtually guarantees that boldly biting fish hook themselves.

The rig is assembled around a central core of heavy-duty nylon at least as strong as the shock leader. Knotting inevitably reduces line strength, so for safety it is better to use a paternoster breaking strain 10 percent above that of your shock leader. In practical beach terms that means tying traces in 35–55 pound monofilament to match 3–5 ounce sinkers. Sometimes even stronger line is required to withstand sand abrasion or to stiffen the core so that hook snoods remain separated. Nothing is worse than a paternoster that tangles into a ball of nylon as soon as it hits the seabed.

Hooks are attached to a paternoster core by lengths of nylon called snoods. Length and breaking strain vary with hook specification, bait selection and species likely to attack. There are no definite rules here, and fish themselves switch preferences with time and tide. Work on the

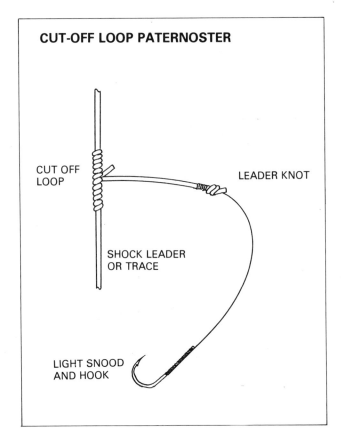

CUT-OFF LOOP PATERNOSTER

CUT OFF LOOP

LEADER KNOT

SHOCK LEADER OR TRACE

LIGHT SNOOD AND HOOK

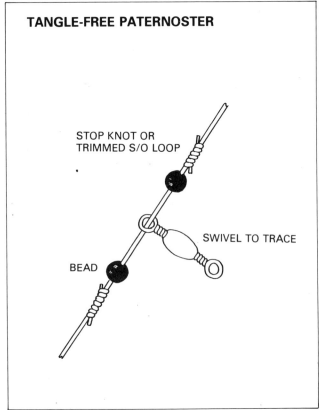

TANGLE-FREE PATERNOSTER

STOP KNOT OR TRIMMED S/O LOOP

SWIVEL TO TRACE

BEAD

principle that if the bait sits neatly on the hook and washes nicely in the tide, any snood is probably good enough. Snoods of 6–15 inch are a reasonable starting point; use 10–20 pound nylon for hooks up to 1/0, and 20–30 pound test for the larger sizes. Sharp teeth obviously require extra trace strength and perhaps even a wire snood.

The number of hooks depends on the length of trace you can handle and the size of fish. There is little point hooking big cod three at a time (even if you were that lucky) but on the other hand a match angler should not waste time snatching single whiting when a 3 hook rig might well attract two or three fish at once.

Pendulum and back casting are the most versatile methods of handling a paternoster because the sinker drop is usually well over 7 feet. Thus a trace up to 6 feet long can be accommodated without fouling the swivel in the rod tip ring or hitting the ground with the sinker; 6 feet allows an easy spread of three 9 inch snoods. Core attachment points are so far apart that hooks and traces never intertwine.

Nearly all paternoster problems are due to the method of tying on snoods. Tangles are the major fault, but strength is involved as well. Paternosters wrongly tied in even 60 pound nylon can snap in mid cast with potentially lethal results. A 5 ounce sinker whistling down the beach is no joke.

The plain stand-off loop is a valuable knot for general purpose fishing. Easy to tie, reasonably strong and adjustable for length, if offers an instant attachment point for snoods. You can tie a 3 hook paternoster in 2 minutes.

The loop itself stands off at right angles from the paternoster core and in heavy monofilament is stiff enough to support and hook. Extra stiffening may be necessary and is best achieved by cutting plastic sleeves 0.25 in longer than the loop and slipping them over it. The extra quarter inch supports the snood knot and prevents its swivelling out of alignment. Old Biro refills, stripped electrical flex and model aeroplane fuel tube are effective stiffeners. 1–3 inch loops are about right for most rigs.

Cut stand-off loops. Heavy nylon is stiff enough in itself to support a lightweight hook, snood and bait. Snip the top half of an ordinary loop about 0.25 inches from the knot coils. Straighten the stand-off section of nylon and tie on the snood with a shock leader knot. Snood and cut loop stand well away from the centre core, and the rig is adequately strong for most species of fish up to 5 pounds. Bait presentation is particularly neat with

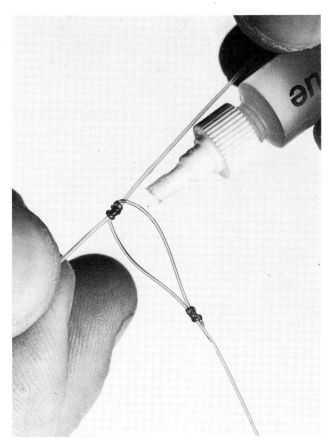

Uni-knot snood tied directly to the leader and super-glued in place.

Aberdeen Blue hooks. Tangles are virtually eliminated in snoods less than 9 inches long.

Tangle-free casting of long snoods is a little more difficult. You could consider a swivelling rig which, although more expensive and slower to tie does offer one of the best solutions to the eternal problems of big baits cast on 12 inch-plus snoods. Two or three hook paternosters are made this way, but for cod and big bass it is better to use one bait.

Method A
Tie a 5 or 6 turn stand-off loop at the correct height on the centre core. Cut off the loop to leave just the knot barrel. Slide on a small bead, a swivel, then a second bead. Sandwich the beads and swivel with a second cut-down loop tied about 2 inches from the first. Knot barrels prevent the beads from sliding out of position, and beads buffer line from swivel pressure when a fish takes hold. Snoods and hooks are the same as for a normal paternoster rig.

Method B
Two knots in the paternoster core must introduce weakness. Very powerful casters are acutely aware of a potential snap-off. Instead of tying and cutting stand-off loops, they retain beads and swivel with two separate nylon stop-knots bound tightly to the

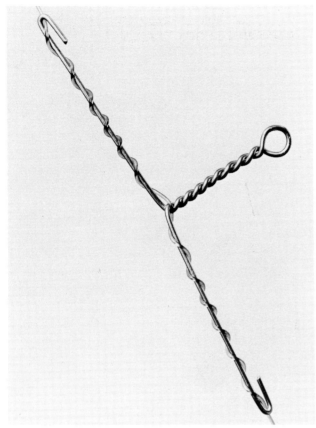

Simple wire boom twisted from stainless steel wire.

heavy core and usually further secured by a dribble of superglue. At worst, the stoppers slip under heavy pressure—a small price to pay for extra insurance against killing your neighbour.

Wire booms twisted on to the paternoster are the old fashioned way to attach snoods. The main objection is excessive air resistance, but there are small diameter stainless steel wire booms on sale that minimise the risk. Some booms have attachment points for the snood, others are purely supportive—the snood is still tied to the paternoster core. On the whole, you would do better not to bother about booms except for flounder and dab fishing, where for some reason they sometimes appear to increase the catch.

Bare snoods may be tied direct to the paternoster core. Most good knots will suffice, but there is a special system based on the Uni-knot which produces a neat stand-off. Tie the snood to the core with a Uni-knot, and be sure to leave a spare end of line at least 4 inches long. Tie this free end back against the main snood with another Uni-knot. A type of triangular boom results, stiff enough to support hook and baits. The snood slips under high pressure, but you can avoid most problems by gluing the first Uni-knot to the heavy nylon. The rig is extremely cheap to make and

therefore ideal for rough ground fishing where tackle losses are high.

Keeping baits on

All terminal rigs tend to rip off baits in mid cast. Paternosters are worse than most because they are the best rig for long distance work and thus subjected to higher stress. In standard form with snoods dangling, any rig will smash soft baits to pieces. Bait clips and snood restraints are essential for top results. These two accessories are so important that many anglers incorporate them in every trace they tie. For what little it costs, why do less?

Bait clips are blunt, shallow hooks which strap to the paternoster core and interlock with the baited hook for casting. The distance between hook and clip is adjusted so that the arrangement holds together while the rig is held straight by the sinker's weight but unfastens when the core buckles in contact with the sea. Anchored close to the terminal rig throughout the cast, baits are less likely to tangle and burst. Reduced air drag adds many yards to the cast—as much as 10 percent with bulky tackle.

Bait clips are made from a scrap of stainless steel wire or cut-down hooks. Either whip the shank to the paternoster core or fix it on with a piece of

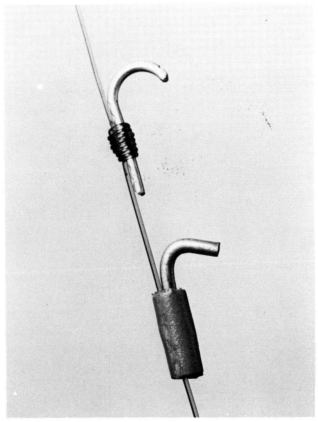

Examples of bait clips. The top clip is cut from a DCA sinker loop; the other is bent from scrap brass wire. Whippings are more secure, but plastic sleeves allow instant adjustment.

rubber tube just large enough in diameter to accept heavy nylon and wire clip with a firm push fit. The clip should be free to slide under moderate pressure so that you can adjust the interlocked hooks to a suitable pressure. Trial and error is the only way to find the best settings for clip and snoods. One clip is required for each snood on the paternoster. Fix the baits up or down the trace as you prefer. The best in-flight position for a single bait is just behind the sinker.

Tying on sinker and leader

Knotting a trace directly to sinker and leader is bad practice. Knots tend to slip under full-power casting pressure, and the sinker knot is wide open to seabed abrasion. After three of four casts and retrieves over sand and shingle, a direct sinker knot is too weak to withstand one more big cast.

Swivels and split rings are ideal intermediary links. Either is acceptable. Split rings are cheap, reliable and very strong. Swivels are probably unnecessary in general surf angling even with fixed spool reels which twist line. Very few if any swivels comb out twists. Most of them are little more than expensive substitutes for a split ring, and less reliable.

If you must use swivels, buy the best: Dexter and Berkeley are as good as any. Swivels 0.5—1

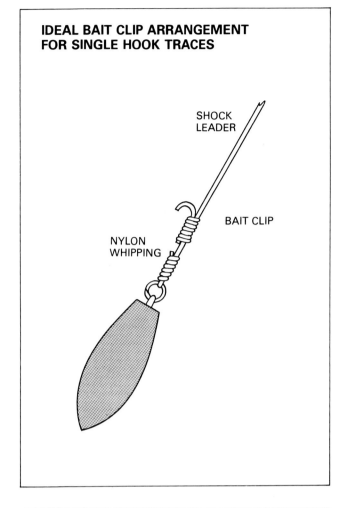

IDEAL BAIT CLIP ARRANGEMENT FOR SINGLE HOOK TRACES

SHOCK LEADER

BAIT CLIP

NYLON WHIPPING

Dexter swivel with detachable loop for rapid trace changing.

Stainless steel split ring and Palomar knot ensure firm sinker attachment and safe casting.

101

inch long are suitable for all-round beach work. Which split rings? Mustad Ovals 0.375–0.75 inches long are superior to any other. Guard against cheap rings that pull open under moderate pressure. The same goes for link swivels: most of them are bad news, and the worst are potential killers. Some Oriental link swivels of the safety pin type burst open at 10 pounds pressure.

A plastic-sleeved knot is an acceptable alternative for sinker attachment. Mould your sinkers with narrow tail loops. Thread an inch of rubber tube on to the lower end of the terminal rig, tie the nylon straight to the sinker loop, then pull the tube down to cover the knot barrel and wire. The sleeve buffers line and knot from seabed abrasion, eliminating the need for a swivel or split ring. Long-tail sinker wires can be bent into a tight 'U'

instead of a closed loop, then tied the same way. With the sleeve in place, there is no danger of the knot slipping free.

Quick-change attachments are standard equipment in match fishing. Two traces are used, one on the rod, the other prebaited and hung on the rod rest. Instead of rebaiting the original trace when you retrieve it—with or without fish on the end—unclip the whole rig, replace it with the spare one, and re-cast immediately. Fresh baits are back in the water within seconds. Time saved means more fish caught, especially when fish swim downtide in small shoals which may be in casting range for only 10 minutes at a time.

A plain swivel on the end of a leader, plus a safety-pin link clip on each end of the trace work

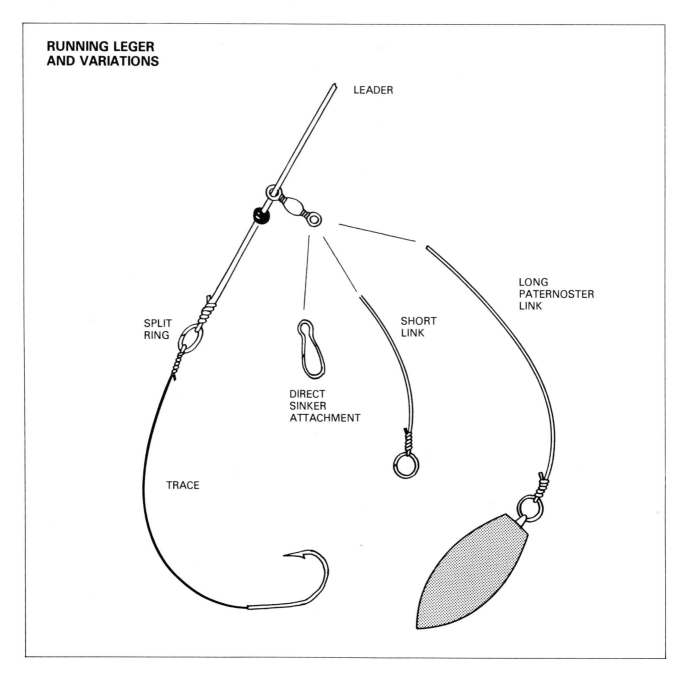

RUNNING LEGER AND VARIATIONS

LEADER

SPLIT RING

DIRECT SINKER ATTACHMENT

SHORT LINK

LONG PATERNOSTER LINK

TRACE

well enough. Check the quality of the components before you start to cast big sinkers at full power. Even better are the new detachable swivels marketed by Dexter Products. One loop lifts out of the swivel barrel. One swivel and two spare ends serves the same purpose as conventional quick release gadgets and are much stronger and safer.

Snood stoppers are a neat way to prevent baits slipping from the hook and up the snood towards the stand-off loop. Most baits slip under full casting power and even bait clips cannot save them. In fact, clips aggravate the situation. Whip a few turns of stiff nylon to the snood just above the hook, trim the rear end short and leave the other—the one nearer the hook—about 0.25 inches long. Worms and other baits skidding up the shank are trapped by the whisker of free nylon. If a high proportion of your bites never develop into hooked fish, bait slip may well be the reason.

Specialised traces

Running legers are a waste of time and money for general surfcasting. The theory of a free-running trace is defeated by distance and tidal current; and most fish take paternostered baits equally well anyway. Short range fishing for rays and conger

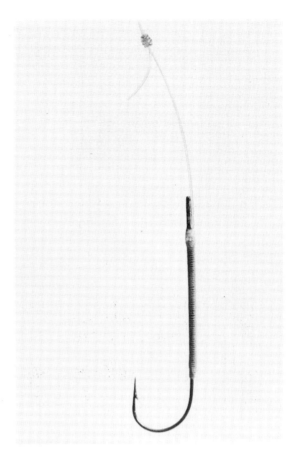

A whisker of stiff nylon tied above the hook prevents bait slip and missed bites.

eels are the main exception. Here, delicacy of presentation is boosted by a straight through trace and a sliding sinker.

Complicated and expensive booms like Clements and Kilmore are unnecessary. Thread a plain swivel on to the leader, then connect trace to leader with a second swivel or a split ring. Attach the sinker to the sliding swivel and your rig is complete. Sinkers are either hitched on with a link clip or split ring, or simply tied on with a short insert of nylon monofilament. If you are worried about the sliding swivel digging into the trace swivel knot, keep them apart with a nylon bead.

Running legers are more useful when modified for specialist work. On rough ground, tie the sinker to its swivel with weak nylon. If a sinker fouls the bottom its weak link, called a rotten bottom, breaks first. Sometimes it operates like a dream; as often as not the hook snags instead, in which case you lose the lot. A rotten bottom is most useful when the sinker snags after a fish is hooked. Snap off the weak nylon and resume the battle.

Shorten the trace, extend the nylon link between sinker and slider, and you are back to the tangle-free paternoster theme. A free-running trace is unimportant in most circumstances, but its swivel does prevent tangles. There is no great

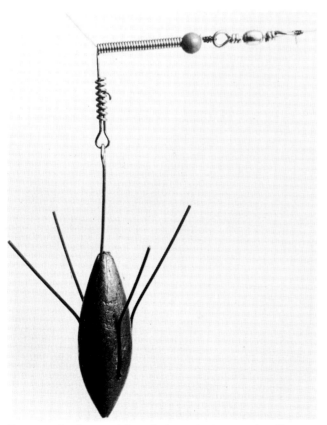

Home-made clips or plain swivels are just as good as the traditional booms and much cheaper.

advantage in doing it this way, but it does mean you can change from a running trace to a paternoster in seconds. For hard casting the nylon link must be at least the same breaking strain as the leader itself.

Very long traces rigged paternoster or running style are sometimes useful for shy-feeding species or for presenting baits just off the bottom. Under normal conditions it is impossible to cast a 10 or 12 foot trace. But if you rig 2 bait clips on the leader, say 6 feet apart and facing away from each other, a long trace can be taken over the top clip and the baited hook fixed below. Both clips release when the sinker hits the water, and the whole trace floats cleanly into the tide. If necessary buoy the hook with a sliver of cork or polystyrene foam. At least it holds the crabs at bay.

Knots for trace assembly and general fishing

New knots appear every season. Most claims are wildly exaggerated, and after a few months everyone returns to the old faithfuls—blood knots, leader knots, bimini twists, palomars and uni-knots. As I have already explained, ease of tying and reproducibility are just as important as ultimate tensile strength. In my view there is a lot of nonsense written about knots, and I sometimes wonder why so many writers set themselves up as knot experts. For the money I suppose.

Anyway, I have deliberately cut the list to the bone. All these knots are perfectly safe for surf fishing. If one fails, the reason is either lack of practice on your part, or some failure in the line. Perhaps the sharp edge of a swivel or seabed abrasion had already damaged the nylon. It is true that some knots are stronger under laboratory conditions, but here we are solely concerned with the reality of surf fishing.

All these knots stand up to the rigours of casting and fishing, but wouldn't it be nice if one knot could handle everything—reel line, leader, traces and hooks? Try working out your tackle on the Uni-knot system. You may be convinced, as I am, that it really is the universal nylon monofilament hitch.

Blood knot

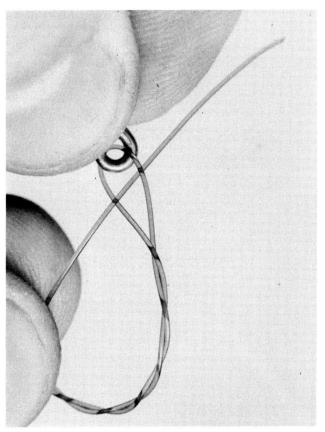

Blood knot 1. *Push the line through the ring and double back about 4 inches. Twist the strands around each other six times and push the spare end through the formed loop.*

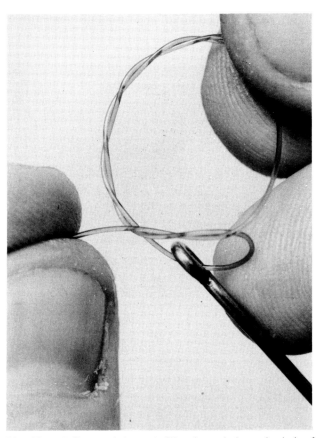

Blood knot 2. *Now tuck the end of line through the main circle of the knot.*

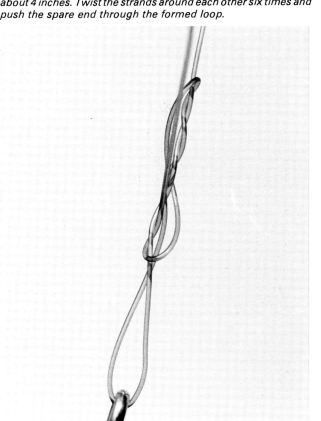

Blood knot 3. *Pull gently on the knot until the coils fall neatly in place. Then lick the knot to lubricate the material. Friction burns dry line.*

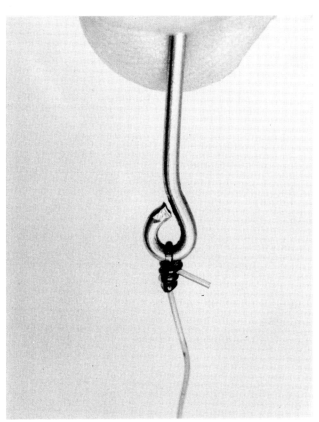

Blood knot 4. *Pull the knot tight and trim off the end. Leave about 0.125 inches free in case the knot slips under pressure.*

Leader knot

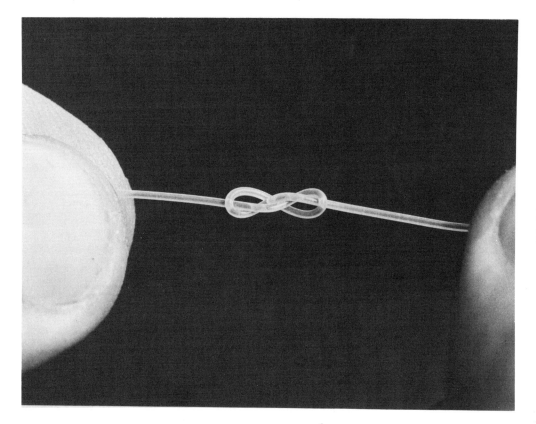

Leader knot 1. *Tie a half hitch in the leader and pull it tight enough to form a figure eight.*

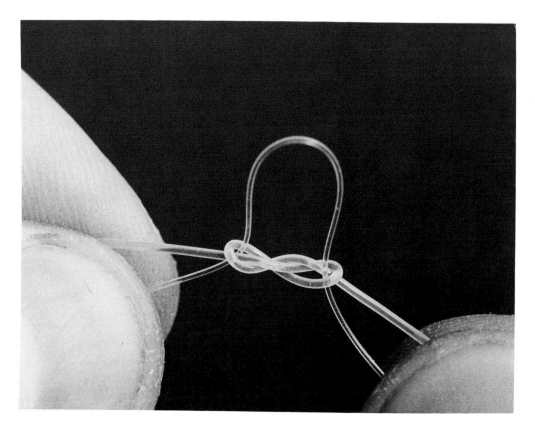

Leader knot 2. *Push the main line through the figure eight. Notice that the main line feeds in and out parallel with the ends of the leader itself, not on the opposite side of the loops.*

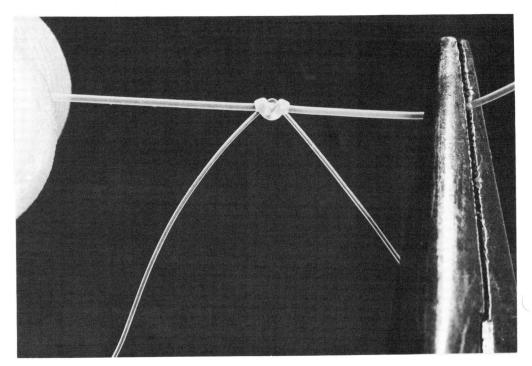

Leader knot 3. Pull the leader hitch tight with pliers.

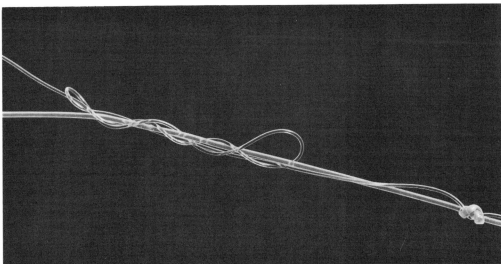

Leader knot 4. Tie a Uni-knot in the main line. Pull it tight enough to settle the coils. Then slide it up to the other knot.

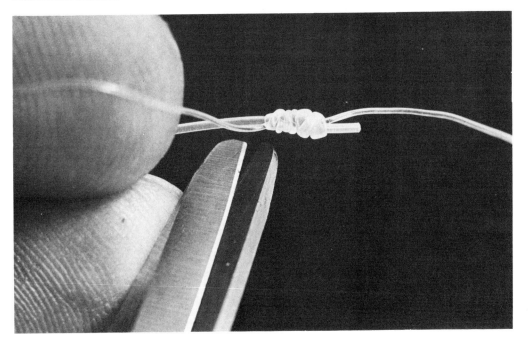

Leader knot 5. Pull the two knots snugly against each other and trim the ends. The Uni-knot is trimmed quite close but the leader end is left 0.125 inches long to insure against slipping.

Uni-knot

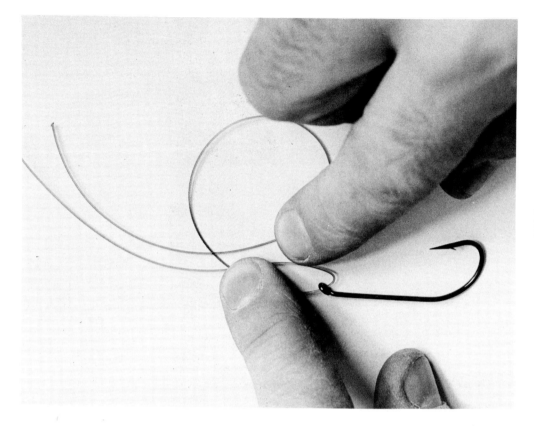

Uni-knot 1. *Pass six inches of line through the eye, double it over, then form a loop.*

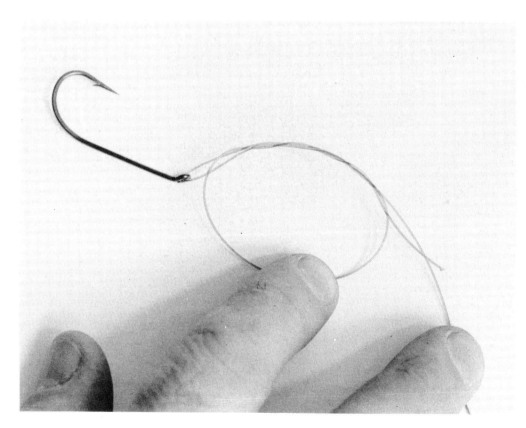

Uni-knot 2. *Lay the loop next to the main part of the line. Wrap the spare end of nylon around the two parallel sections of line. Use at least six full turns.*

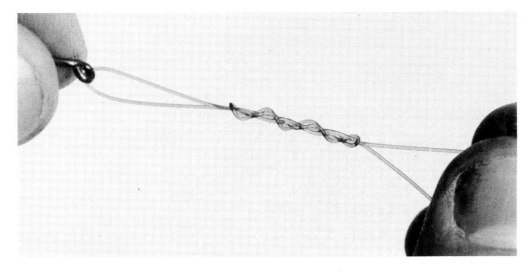

Uni-knot 3. Pull the ends of the line to form the knot barrel. When the coils fall into place, lick them and pull the knot tighter.

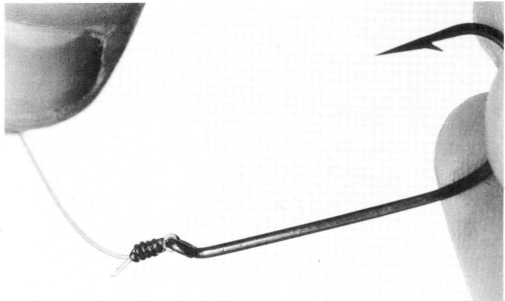

Uni-knot 4. Slide the knot close to the hook eye, then pull fully tight. The Uni-knot is also excellent for tying together two pieces of nylon.

Uni-knot 5. Tightening the coils slightly away from the lure attachment eye forms a secure loop of nylon which enhances underwater action.

Stand-off loop

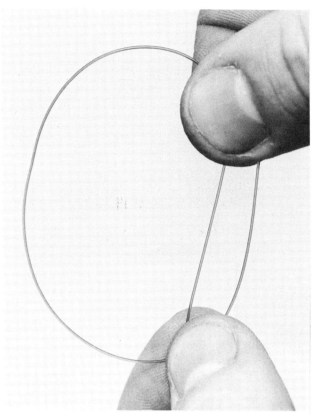

Stand-off loop 1. *Form a loop in the trace at the appropriate point for snood attachment.*

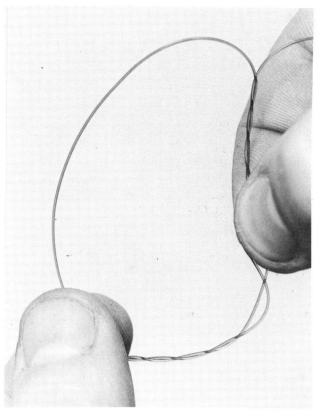

Stand-off loop 2. *Twist the parallel strands around each other six or seven times.*

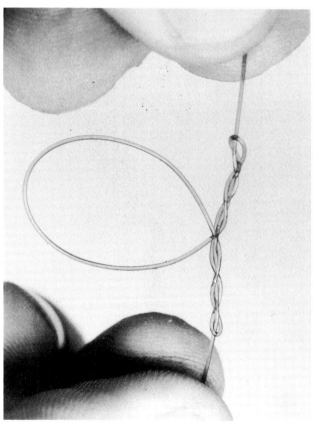

Stand-off loop 3. *Push the opposite side of the main loop through the middle of the twisted section and gently pull the coils into place.*

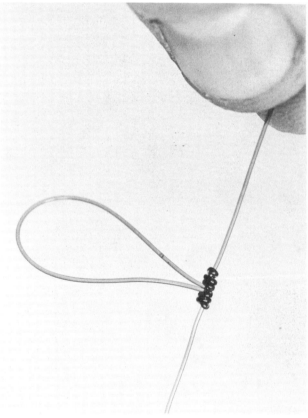

Stand-off loop 4. *Tighten the knot after lubricating the nylon to avoid friction burns. Stand-off loops sometimes slip so much that the loop disappears. Put in plenty of twists, and tighten the knot very slowly. Some brands of nylon skid worse than others.*

Palomar knot

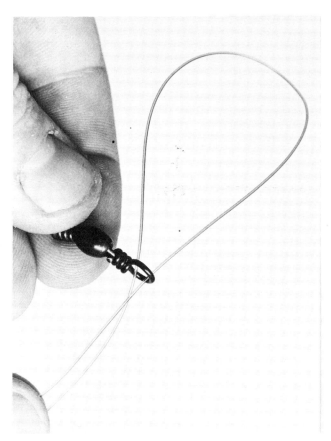

Palomar knot 1. Double 6 inches of line and push into the swivel loop.

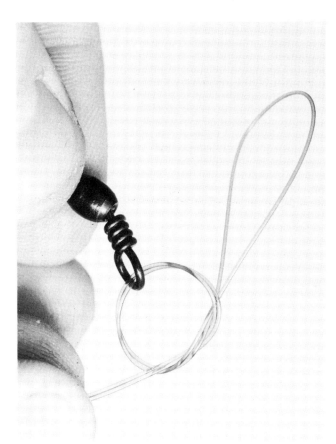

Palomar knot 2. Tie a half hitch, and make sure that the loop is big enough to slip around the lure, sinker, hook or whatever.

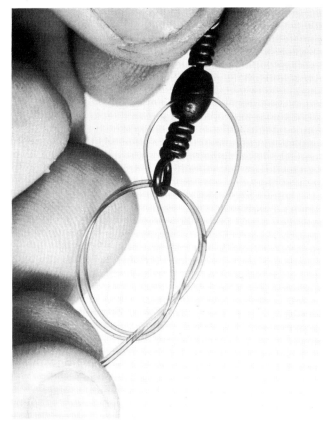

Palomar knot 3. Pass the loop around the swivel, then gently draw the knot tight. The coils must pull down evenly or the knot slips.

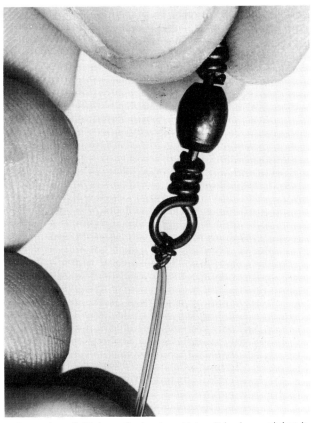

Palomar knot4. Tighten the knot and trim. It looks weak but is actually one of the strongest monofilament knots.

Index